# Heart & Soul Poems

# Heart & Soul Poems

by

Shirley Ann Wood

Order this book online at www.trafford.com
or email orders@trafford.com

Most Trafford titles are also available at major online book retailers.

Printed in the United States of America.

ISBN: 978-1-4269-5202-9 (sc)
ISBN: 978-1-4269-5203-6 (hc)
ISBN: 978-1-4269-5204-3 (e)

Library of Congress Control Number: 2010918547

*Trafford rev. 12/27/2010*

 www.trafford.com

**North America & International**
toll-free: 1 888 232 4444 (USA & Canada)
phone: 250 383 6864 ✦ fax: 812 355 4082

# FOREWORD

The poems that are included in this manuscript are a collection of writings that I started when I was very young. I became inspired to write these poems by the events that I experienced as I was growing up. I am still writing poems at the age of 82, and will continue as long as I am able.

Over the years I have had great feedback from many readers. This has inspired me to have my poems in print for others to enjoy. I would be more than pleased to know that my poems have inspired or brought comfort to those that will read them.

I have separated my works into two manuscripts one with the title "Heart & Soul" Poems, and the other titled "Faith & Hope" Poems. I have a strong Christian belief and therefore many of my poems, especially the poems included in the Faith & Hope manuscript, will reflect this.

These poems are appropriate for readers of all ages and hopefully will be an inspiration for all that read them.

# Contents

# ABSENTIA

*He went away that summers day*

*Saying he'd return no more*

*Long years ago he'd gone away–*

*Turned his back, until the day*

*He decided that he loved her,*

*All would be upon her as it was before*

*He called her name, but all in vain–*

*She didn't live there anymore!*

*So he went looking for her,*

*He would find her–He was sure!*

*But everyone, he asked, just said–*

*She never comes here anymore!*

*Then one night as he sat drinking*

*Out there dancing on the floor–*

*Suddenly he saw the one–*

*That he'd been searching for*

*He went to her–said dance with me*

*And he held her–as before–*

*But now–The one he'd left behind*

*Didn't live there anymore!*

# ACCEPTANCE

*I have loved so many people, oh so very much,*

*With all my heart and all my life, & yes my very soul*

*But I have learned as years went by–*

*Not to tell them so.*

*You tell them that you love them*

*When they seem to have a need,*

*Otherwise, you wait, you hope,*

*And sometimes - you recede-*

*To a place that's set apart-*

*It's called your place*

*Within their minds*

*No place within their hearts - Until!*

*They have nobody else*

*Who ever seems to care-*

*And then - once more - they'll beckon-*

*Just to have somebody there !*

*Then you will do! Ah yes you !*

*Can you believe that this is true?*

*That now you are accepted-*

*You can become a part-*

*Of what you always wanted*

*A place within their heart.*

*They open wide the portals*

*That you may step inside*

*But if you do-*

*Remember you-*

*Always will abide-*

*Within the realm of what they feel*

*What they think and do,*

*And someday - you could vanish*

*Every single bit of you*

*And from the ashes, could arise*

*What you were never meant to be*

*A Phoenix of the one, you loved*

*With their exact identity*

*Imprinted with their thoughts and actions*

*With all their hopes and dreams*

*Working for the goals they want*

*involved in all their schemes*

*You lose the way you meant to go*

*For they mean more than you,*

*You have no time left over*

*to Do what you should do !*

*Ah well - that's - life. The way it is !*

*Do they not tell you so?*

*So go to hell - or go your way !*

*Ah ! Lord! Which way to go?*

# ALL I KNOW

*If I could teach you all I know*

*And in some ways show–*

*You how I learned so much*

*It would mean absolutely nothing!*

*For he who thinks that he is*

*Wise should look inside*

*Look at the skies, and ponder*

*Well–*

*For never in "Ten" lifetimes*

*Could we know enough to tell–*

*You how to think–*

*"Your" wisdom comes from deep inside*

*Formed from what you hear*

*And touch, smell and see–*

*All or any one of these–*

*Will lead you to decide*

*What you wish to keep or throw away*

*And as you grow, your choices*

*Will make you who you are from day to day*

*Should you decide at any time*

*You do not want to be–*

*The way you are–*

*Then simply change your mind*

And go as far as your imagination dares

One word of caution–

All must be done thru love of what you do

By a soul that cares

Seek out others of your kind

Those of gentle mind – and

Tender touch who lift you up

And would never crush your–

Fragile hopes and dreams–

They are "The Creators"

Beware the ones who scheme

Then like alligators–

Intent on what they want – devour you

All you try to do


## ALL IS WELL

Unicorns and carousels

Ferris wheels and wishing wells

Fairy tales and make-believe

The practice never to deceive

Rainbows – never- never land–

Where all who live – "Love" – "understand"

God's in his heaven - all is well–

For those who <u>love</u> – there is no hell!

All this! And more! Throughout my life–

As daughter – Sister – friend and wife–

"I have believed" with all my soul–

But that was, "Ah! – so long ago –"

But why? Cannot – I yet let go?

Of all that's <u>proved</u> – "To be not so!"

Could it be? I am misplaced?

Unlike the others of my race

I'm just a thought that's gone astray?

And perhaps – when ere the day–

God smiles – and sets me free!

I'll <u>find</u> – "in never- never land"–

What <u>now</u>! Can never be!

Ah –Twill be good to be back home!

I! Nevermore shall leave–

To live with mortals of such kiln!

Who <u>never</u>! Can believe!!!


## ALL MY CHILDREN

Sweet tender child that delights my eye

Flesh of my flesh – your face, forever etched upon my
immortal soul.

Love so great I weep, for as I hold the soft loveliness of you
within my arms

*I see the future – near – so near, when I must let you go*

*The paths you walk will be your choice*

*For your soul is free – God given to you alone*

*And I can partake of only what <u>you</u> choose to share with me*

*But know that I am here, to comfort – to help to love – I care*
<u>so much</u>!

*But if I give, so do I receive!*

*For as the sun warms the earth – your love warms my heart*
with a tender touch

*You give meaning to my life. Could I but open <u>up</u> my heart,*

*You'd find that you're a part of every breath I take!*

*I delight in all your joys and victories*

*And hurt as you do with every painful mistake*

*But caring, I must hold your love with open hand*

*Lest I crush the fragile Beauty that is you!*

*So Dear Heart heed your own good counsel,*

*Find all the Happiness you can, and be kind in all you do!!*

## ALWAYS THERE

*If I should go–where you can't follow,*

*Look within your heart!*

*There–you'll find in Memories*

*Of which I am a part*

*Funny things, to make you smile,*

*Perhaps a tear or two,*

*Tender moments, full of love*

*When I was close to you!*

*Magic moments, full of wonder!*

*Times we disagreed*

*In each and every moment*

*There always was a need*

*Just–to have each other,*

*Just to feel and care,*

*To know what ere the moment,*

*We were always there!*

*I for you–you for me,*

*So it was, and is*

*Because we love each other*

*We take, withhold, or give.*

*We somehow think, there is no death!*

*And we are right–that's true!*

*For you'll live on, when I am gone*

*And I'll live on thru you!*

*Even after eons pass, and there's no memory*

*Of what I was, and how I lived,*

*And none remember me*

*It does not matter–I was here!*

*So I shall always be!*

A thousand–yes ten thousand years

Whatever be the time

There'll be many children

From this seed of mine!

Each one unique! God's glory!

And thru his love, you see


## AWARE

In winter – walk along a lowly strip of sand,

Look upwards to infinity on a clear dark silent night

Ponder the words of Holy Men as you clasp a loved one's
Hand

Drink in the sweet essence of flowers in bloom

Imagine your mind, like wild birds in flight

Bask in the warmth of the summer sun

Press on thru the driving rain

Run with the wind, sit by a stream,

So exploring-then come back again-

Each day-each night so different

Yet somehow much the same

Tragedy and laughter, summer, fall

Winter, spring, happiness and pain,

A child, a youth, adult, old-age

All one yet each one changed

*Like days and nights so different*

*Yet somehow much the same*

*All you see, smell, hear and touch,*

*All others experience too*

*Some learn little others much*

*What will the world teach you?*

*Open your mind the whole world's there*

*Bequeathed to the ones who love and care.*

## BENJAMIN

*Benjamin was crying*

*How could I stop his tears*

*Mend his tiny broken heart*

*Dispel his childish fears?*

*His great dark eyes beseeched me*

*Please Grandmum – Is it true?*

*There's no such thing as magic*

*And Santa's Dad or you?*

*There's no Easter Bunny*

*To bring eggs on Easter Day*

*And there're no magic places*

*Where elves and fairies play?*

*You always said*

*These things were so*

*And my mom says it too*

*But all the kids say it's a lie*

*And none of it is true!*

*Benjamin, come here love*

*Sit on Grandmum's knee*

*Look out thru the window*

*Tell me what you see!*

*He looked and starting naming*

*All that he could see*

*The flowers in my garden*

*A cloud, a bird, a tree*

*A little dog, two kittens*

*A lake, a butterfly*

*And arching over all*

*A rainbow in the sky*

*Good, Ben, you've noticed lots of things*

*But there's much more by far*

*Sunlight chasing shadows*

*Nighttime lit by stars*

*About a trillion magic things*

*But listen now*

*It's true*

*The greatest magic in this world*

*Is someone just like you*

*All the love within your heart*

*The dreams within your mind*

*That makes you want great wondrous things*

*And if you'll seek you'll find*

*That there are Easter bunnies*

*Elves and fairies too*

*And if you're good at Christmas*

*Santa comes to you*

*For God made you*

*With love, Ben dear*

*Just the way you are*

*And because He loved you so*

*Once upon a Star*

*He sent His own beloved Son*

*Who was a lot like you*

*For He believed in magic*

*And dreams that could come true!*

*He said we could move mountains*

*If we could just believe*

*With such a little*

*Bit of faith*

*Small as a mustard seed*

*Talk about imagination*

*Do you believe that's true?*

*Well Ben – It is!*

*I've seen them moved*

*And someday so will you*

*And if you keep the magic*

*"Of Believing"*

*In each single thing you do*

*There isn't <u>anything</u> you'll ask*

*That God won't give to you!*

*So don't listen to the Blind ones*

*The ones who <u>will</u> not see*

*The magic that is everywhere*

*For them, for you, for me*

*Just because they do not see it*

*Doesn't mean it isn't so*

*For Jesus said it's everywhere*

*And for certain*

*He would know*

*And there are <u>other</u> wonders*

*Ones we've yet to see*

*So many more that it will take*

*A whole Eternity*

*For God to show us*

*All the things He has in store*

*Ah , yes, Ben there <u>is</u> magic*

*And More*

*Thru love*

*Much more!*

## BEYOND

*Beyond the Memory of Mankind*

*Beyond the borders of their minds*

*Lies a Realm that's free of Sin*

*That in a few, still dwells within*

*Struggling against all pride*

*Seeks to emerge*

*From deep inside*

*To spread its wings*

*In truth's pure light*

*Rejecting lies that Curse the Night.*

*Night of Angels and of Man*

*Hiding knowledge of the plan*

*Of what we are to be*

*Pitting one against the other*

*So we might not be free*

*"Fear" – the weapon used to bind*

*"Fear" – that infiltrates each mind*

*"Fear" – that keeps us from each dream*

*And alters truths that might be seen*

That could set us free

"Fear" – the lie, illusion, tangling you and me

In a web that binds us to our mortality

Yet before the flesh

We were Spirit pure

And when the flesh is gone

We shall be spirit as before!

So truly we are Spirit Beings

And should think accordingly

Instead of Petty Thoughts and Stupid Rivalry.

## BIG BUSINESS

How many science-fiction stories have we read?

Of alien invaders that filled our souls with dread?

Of battles over planet Earth, Our home! So fair and green,

Of how, with great nobility, the greatest ever seen–

We fought, with monumental courage – to save our planet Earth,

From ones who might pollute and kill – everything of worth!

Then as the tale continues, we hold our loved ones near,

To protect their lives, their heritage - no sacrifice too dear,

Great heads of state, science, churches, ordinary man–

Combine their efforts and their strengths to devise a plan–

To drive off these great invaders – with minds as dark as sin,

*Then as the story closes – we devise a way ! And <u>Win</u>!*

*But what of "Another Story" – We read about each day?*

*N<u>ot</u> aliens, but "Business Men", who want to have their way*

*Sweeping <u>clean</u> our mountains – for timber growing there,*

*Belching from their factories, pollutants in our air,*

*Sending forth great tankers, containing oil so thick–*

*That should they sink – there is no way to clean the filthy slick,*

*Leveling rain forests, with ought a second thought*

*Of all the precious lifeforms that die forever, or get caught,*

*In ever closing circles, until finally one day–*

*They'll have no place to go, no place left to stay.*

*But perhaps, there'll be No One! – left, on planet Earth*

*When "aliens" (Our Businessmen) have killed all things of worth*

*Right now! Our ozone layer brings warnings that are dire–*

*And as the Bible has predicted–*

*Our world <u>could end in fire</u>!*

*L<u>ess</u> than a hundred years ago – we used to bask and play,*

*Beneath the sun that gave Earth life,*

*But what of us today?*

*We <u>need</u> great heads of state, churches, science, man–*

*To combine their strengths, their efforts to devise a plan,*

*That will <u>stop</u> these great destroyers with minds as dark as sin,*

*Take steps to <u>heal</u> our wounded Earth*

*Before – – "No Body" Wins!*

## BLUE EGYPTIAN SKIES

*On a Pyramid they Stood*

*"Neath Blue Egyptian Skies*

*Mighty Priest and Protégé-*

*While on the Altar Lie-*

*A form so still - so innocent-*

*Of very tender years*

*Drugged - To erase - from form and face*

*All signs of Dreadful fears-*

*Towards this day - The Protégé*

*Intent on Her own will*

*Had studied neath the Evil Priest*

*Mastering each Skill*

*Marduk - The Priest had not a qualm*

*For he had taught her well –*

*Did not suspect that Heaven's forces soon would Battle Hell*

*He lifted high the dagger - then placed it in her hand*

*She held it toward the people of the Pharaoh's land*

*Then she spoke - As Marduk Stood - in Utter Consternation*

*Gathering her forces now - She made her Proclamation!*

*All Human Sacrifice would cease - forward - from this day*

*She sheathed the Dagger - Threw it high - and as it spun away*

*She turned to face the might foe - As from the populace below*

*Stunned silence - then a murmur - swelled to a mighty Sound*

*As they watched the Clash of Wills high above the ground*

*Long - and great the battle as Back and forth it went*

*Wounding - Wounded - Drenched in sweat - Both forces almost spent-*

*In her pain she raised her eyes - to the Blue Egyptian Skies-*

*In a foreign tongue she spoke - as all the power she invoked- Gathered overhead-*

*One last great Clash as lightening flashed*

*Then the Priest Lay dead*

*But it had drained her far too much-*

*As tenderly she bent to touch and lift the lovely Child*

*Life forces left her body - still she gently smiled*

*She was the Victor - It was done! Against dark forces she had Won*

*And tho it cost her life - He Effort would be honoured- By - no more sacrifice!*

*They placed the dagger in her hand*

*In Sheath of Jewels Rare-*

*Never to be used again - Or for those who'd Dare*

*The Wrath of Heaven would decent on the Pharaoh's land-*

*And - In the bolt of lightening*

*A swift avenging hand-*

*Protector of the innocent - in Hieroglyphics bold-*

*is the Record of that Day-*

*And Warning plainly Told!*

## CEASED TO BE

*Once – You were my world*

*But it just wouldn't do*

*Because I meant little or*

*Nothing to you!*

*My love and my friendship*

*You counted upon*

*But when I needed you*

*You weren't there – you had gone*

*Gone to another – I couldn't believe*

*I felt so betrayed – so hurt – so deceived*

*How could this be? I searched deep inside*

*For a reason to live. Now that love was denied*

*Gone forever – in time – the World I called you*

*No where to turn – nothing to do*

*Except to rebuild – in my heart and my mind*

*A new world for me – where maybe, in time*

*I'll mean more than nothing – to someone – somewhere*

*Once again learn to live – to laugh – and to share*

*Once again feel the sun, learn how to be*

*Important at last – because I am me!*

*I'll never forget what I've learned – that is true*

*But you're wrong when you say – I don't forgive you*

*You were my world*

*What more can I say?*

*We cannot return- for like yesterday*

*It dwells in a time we'll never more see*

*It's not unforgiveness – it's just ceased to be!*

## CHAMELEON

*I am a chameleon – have you heard of such a thing?*

*Never in their whole long life can a chameleon sing,*

*Never can they dream a dream, or ever learn to fly–*

*So earthbound are they – they don't know – there even is a sky.*

*They simply crawl from place to place*

*Hiding from the human race–*

*And others of their kind – and if they even think at all–*

*All that's in their mind–*

*Is to adjust and to survive – and to do that – stay alive–*

*They change their body hue – to look like their surroundings,*

*So that I, and you – will not discover they are there–*

*Taking space – breathing air, being what they are*

*Unaware that there are those – who wish upon a Star–*

*Yes! I am a chameleon – tho I've never wished to be,*

*Others – they are human – but it seems my destiny–*

*Was <u>not</u> to be all I could be – for when I even dared–*

*I was per se – unorthodox – and so nobody cared–*

*Indeed there were objections – To the person known as me–*

*You're too different – they all screamed – you have no <u>right</u>*

*to be*

*So I changed all I was, took on different hues–*

*Becoming first like this one – then like you , and you!*

*Why? To survive? Stay alive? It didn't work that way,*

*Adjusting to each person's whim – the penalty I paid–*

*Was instead of being human – I've become "A thing!"*

## THE <u>CHANGELING</u>

*There was a time when I could see*

*With wondrous Childish clarity*

*The stars that were placed there just for me,*

*The sun that warmed, that laughed and danced*

*The stream that tinkled, the wind that pranced*

*The snow that sparkled like a magic thing,*

*The grass that rippled, the wonders of spring*

*The trees that whispered to a summer breeze*

*The brilliant flowers, yes all of these*

*Promised a life so full and rich*

*That I should never ever wish*

*For more, for was there more than this?*

*But now the years have passed me by,*

*And as I gaze at the darkened sky*

*I find the stars are far away.*

*And my vision is blurred as day by day*

*I work and worry my life away*

*For now I am an adult.*

## CHILD OF A DREAM

*Child of the Wind—you fan the flames or race thru a clear*
*blue sky*

*Unpredictable—*

*Always—*

*You refresh and cool,*

*Rampage and scream*

*Whisper softly—or die!*

*And just when the earth thinks you will not move*

*You rise like a nymph from the grave*

*Bend the saplings,*

*Fell the oaks,*

*And anger the ocean waves*

*Trapped in canyons, you wail like a child–*

*Set free you are gentle,*

*With perfume you beguile–lovers–*

*That stroll in the moonlight haze*

*Carry memories of youth–*

*To the lovers of age,*

*Child of the wind full of anger and mirth*

*Coquettishly teasing the children of earth*

*Racing free cross ocean and land*

*Our burdens and pain you don't understand*

*And who can blame you because you are free?*

*You are the child you were meant to be*

*But when you in your vast clear blue sky*

*Are restricted from entering space*

*'Tis then you darken and raindrops cry*

*To be bound, and kept in your place.*

*All things are relative, child of the wind*

*You're the free'est of all–it would seem*

*But there is a child–Not shackled at all*

*Who is known as "The Child of a Dream".*

*She walks the earth or roams the sky*

*No barrier–time or space*

*She lives forever, the eons pass,*

*She's the best of every race.*

*Always gentle, lovely, serene–*

*Her name is Beauty–The Child of A Dream*

*Her sisters are Charity–Hope and Faith*

*Her God is forgiving–Full of Grace*

*A dream she'll tuck within your heart to make you part*

*Of those–who do not know!*

*Such things can not be so*

*Believing you'll go on*

*Defeating all adversity*

*Until the time–that Golden Dawn*

*Your dream becomes reality!*

*And as like begets like*

*Inspiration, it seems–is the seed that gives birth–*

*To A Child of A Dream*

*So her children increase, are found everywhere*

*Changing the lives of those who despair*

*Her Ethereal beauty can never be bound*

*But just hope–for one moment*

*And she'll be around*

*Filling your head with impossible schemes*

*The things she believes in*

*"This Child of a Dream"*

# CHILD OF THE UNIVERSE

*Child of the universe – Searching the earth–*

*For wisdom, for love, for purpose, for worth!*

*Certain, at first – that it's <u>easy</u> to find,*

*Bending our wills – Bending our minds–*

*To creating a world –"As we'd have it be,"*

*Revolving around – just <u>one</u> person – Me!*

*And when things go wrong – we scream – it won't do!*

*It was nothing <u>I</u> did! So the fault rests with <u>you</u>!*

*Then slowly – we learn with the passage of years–*

*Thru error and trials – tribulation and tears–*

*Thru sharing, thru caring, – and happiness too–*

*That the best I am – Is the best that is you*

*And the best that <u>We</u> are – is the best of mankind*

*For <u>all</u> things a reason – a season – a time–*

*For what purpose? God's own! That perhaps if we grow,*

*In the knowledge of love –of creation – we'll <u>know</u>*

*That a child of the universe – must rise above – the*

*Mortal bound body thru faith hope and love–*

*To find the great treasures – no matter the cost*

*The treasures, the wisdom, of Paradise lost–*

*The beginning – the place from whence we once came*

*In the likeness of God – who called us by name–*

*Impossible dream? Impossible task? It would seem*

*to be so – and well you might ask–*

*How can we rise so far above this mortal bound body*

*Through faith, hope and love–*

*To alter what is – to all that "might be"–*

*Combined, we can't do it – let alone Me!*

*Ah but we <u>can</u>, by all that we do–*

*Thru the Spirit – the power – the love given you*

*Why do <u>we</u> not know? Or not even learn*

*What's <u>already</u> ours we <u>don't</u> have to earn*

*And till the day we change, believe in our worth*

*We all remain sinners – children of Earth*

*Destroyers of all – bound by our greed–*

*Screaming in pain – begging in need–*

*Never using the key – given time after time–*

*To the riddle of ages – a life that's divine–*

*Do unto others – and you shall be free–*

*Honor your brother – and you honor Me!*

*Child of the earth – have courage each day*

*K<u>now</u> that I love you – believe what I say–*

*I sacrificed much – thru great agony*

*To redeem you from hell – that you might dwell with me*

*Do not count as treasures – <u>Things</u> of the earth*

*When <u>you</u> are a child – of the universe!*

# CHILDREN OF THE SEA

*We are Newfoundlanders and we shall always be–*

*As we've been in ages past, children of the sea!*

*Tho we've been forbidden to Fish our waters fair*

*Within our hearts and in our souls we always shall be there*

*Ghost ships upon the waters - exploits told in song–*

*Pull us back – just to be out where we belong*

*In a Dory drifting on our beloved sea*

*Where those of greed – not of need*

*Destroyed our legacy*

*Ghost ships upon the waters*

*Exploits told in song*

*Beckon us – come back*

*Come back, back where you belong*

*Where once your people sailed and fished*

*The great Atlantic sea*

*Abundant then and always*

*Thru many centuries*

*Their spirits do not understand*

*Nor indeed, do we*

*How those of greed – not of need*

*Destroyed our legacy*

*Descended from seafarers the mighty men of old*

*Salt for blood, strength of steel*

Shirley Ann Wood

*Adventurous and bold*

*We are Newfoundlanders –*

*And we shall always be*

*As we've been in ages past*

*Children of the sea*

*For centuries we lived along our great Atlantic shores*

*For centuries we've pulled our nets*

*And laid against our oars*

*Now we've been forbidden to fish our waters fair*

*In less than one man's lifetime*

*The fish they say – aren't there*

*Our vessels now are dry – docked*

*And we're told to understand*

*That we must all find other lives*

*No choice – a stern command!*

*No one mentions draggers*

*That ripped the ocean floor,*

*Or tankers with their oil spills*

*Contaminating shores*

*But from a dory – not one cod can be*

*Caught and kept by me*

*While men of greed – not of need*

*Destroy our legacy.*

# THE CIRCLE GAME

*I run in ever tightening circles*

*Nowhere–now–to go,*

*All the things that I once knew–*

*Well now–I just don't know!*

*My mind–a vast confusion*

*And in my soul, it's true*

*The same confusion seems to reign*

*Just don't know what to do!*

*I want the world to simplify*

*Feel like screaming–want to cry*

*Instead I try to keep the pace*

*Knowing that I've lost the race*

*I keep running with the rest*

*Doing what I think is best*

*Hanging on–and on–and on,*

*Thanking God as each days' gone.*

*That someday soon there'll come an end*

*To tears, and fright, and pain,*

*And when it comes–perhaps I'll know–*

*What I once knew–again!*

*Perhaps somewhere, there is a place*

*Where darkness never dwells*

*A warm, and gentle, tender space*

*That has no fear of Hell!*

*Where light is ever present,*

*And love heals every wound,*

*And if there is, I pray, My Lord,*

*To find this place–and soon!*

*For I'm so weary of this game*

*They play on Planet Earth*

*I've known from the beginning*

*The moment of my birth–*

*I was not equipped to play,*

*It all got out of hand.*

*The rules seem all so harsh and cruel*

*Can't seem to understand,*

*So I run in circles, the weak link in the chain*

*Breaking–every now and then–*

*Thus altering–The Game!*

*Then I feel their anger*

*So I withdraw–and hide*

*But they reach in–and draw me out*

*From somewhere deep inside!*

*Insisting that I cannot stay,*

*But try again–to play their way,*

*To please them–I have cried–Please!*

*I have something else to say–*

Try the game–just once, my way.

But they reply, "It cannot be"

Your way is just a fantasy

And you must face reality!

Well I have looked, and I have seen

Reality–is painted green

Green with envy–face obscene

Wearing robes of scarlet red

Dipped in blood of all the dead

Victims of a sinful plan,

Man's inhumanity–to man

And among them, children scream,

You've destroyed our lives, our dreams

Said we were not allowed to be

This–is a reality! The truth I just don't wish to see

Bit it exists–in spite of me!

Why won't they cease this awful game

Full of anger, fear and pain?

A game. That makes each person lose!

When all could win, if they would choose

To care for one another.

Heed the words that Jesus spoke

And make each man their brother!

Make the world a place–God intended it to be,

*Full of love and laughter,*
*And wondrous fantasy!*

## COLOURS

*There Are Unicorns That Play In The Corners Of My Mind*
*And Rainbow Colours Bow To Earth Blessing All Mankind*
*And Yellow Roses Grow Where Sparking Waters' Flow*
*And It Seems That Everywhere Love And Magic Fill The Air*
*Doesn't Anybody Care?*
*The Seasons Come The Seasons Go-*
*God Blesses All So We May Know It's All At His Command*
*Why Do We Scorn His Wonders?*
*And Rape His Holy Land?*
*Why Do We Kill The Babies-*
*As In Herod's Day?*
*Why Do We Curse Our Father In Life?*
*Why Do We Cease To Pray?*
*Are We So Noble And So Free?*
*That We Have Ceased To Care - To Be?*
*The People He Intended?*
*When Jesus Died In Agony*
*So Our Sins Would Be Amended*
*Was This A Waste Of Love Divine?*
*Given For Your Soul And Mine?*

*Are We Greater Now Than He?*

*Do We Take Into Our Hands Our Final Destiny?*

*And If We Do - In Arrogance Why? Cannot, We See-*

*We No Longer Seem To Know The Wonders Of His Earth-*

*No Longer Hold As Holy The Advent Of A Birth,*

*No Longer Care What Others Feel!*

*Just The "I" The "I" - Is Real!*

*The Golden Statue Of Mankind As In Moses Day-*

*Useless And Uncaring With Feet Of Sand Or Clay*

*Still - - - Moses Cared, And Only He!*

*And Perhaps You May Be-*

*The Magic Rainbow Child*

*Who Walks The - Earth In Fantasy - Totally Beguiled-*

*By The Thought Of Unicorns,*

*Possessed By Love So Deep-*

*That Pain Would Wound Your Tender Heart-*

*And Cause You Now To Weep-*

*At The Abortion Of God's Plan*

*Man's Inhumanity To Man*

*Well, If You Do! I Know That You - Must Live In Agony-*

*For Unicorns And Rainbow's Are Not Allowed To Be*

*Like "God" - They Are - "Just Fairy Tales - "*

*A Madman's Fantasy !*

*But Still The Unicorns Do Play*

*In The Corners Of My Mind And Rainbow Colours Bow To*
*The Earth*
*Blessing All Mankind-*
*And I Shall Seek The Rainbow Path-*
*When It's Time For Me To Go Back To The Land Of Magic-*
*Where Yellow Roses Grow-*
*And From The Very Throne Of God-*
*The Living Waters Flow-*
*Tis There Where All Is Love And Grace-*
*I've always Longed To Be A Member Of The Human Race-*
*That Dwells In Fantasy !*
*For It's So Beautiful - Divine, That Locked Within This*
*Heart Of Mine-*
*Is A Longing Just To See-*
*The Beauty That Eludes Mankind-*
*That Was - That Is - Will Be!*
*But I Shall Never Enter In, Unless I'm Cleansed From*
*Mortal Sin-*
*By The "Holy Trinity"*
*So As My Life Comes To A Close*
*I Beg With Head Bowed Low-*
*Look Into This Heart - Tho I Wounded You - Please Know-*
*I Loved You - Loved Your Caring - Loved Your Magic Touch*
*So Please Forgive This Sinner-*
*Who's Loved You - "Oh So Much".*

# CRUEL REALITY

*In the days of make-believe*

*I lived but for while*

*Everyone was sweet and kind.*

*The whole world wore a smile*

*Than I was told a world like this*

*Just wasn't meant to be*

*Grow up they said,*

*And so I did and found reality*

*Reality – the word they use*

*To make you be as they*

*No laughter now, no make-believe*

*No time for fun or play*

*Too bad I lived so little in my time of make-believe*

*I'd go back – but I am blocked*

*By cruel reality!*

# DEAR GENTLE

*Ann - My eternal being*

*You have dwelt with me so long*

*Soft and sweet – Building to a crescendo*

*Then slowly – fading like the last soft notes*

*Of a hauntingly lovely song*

*Vanishing like smoke–*

*And the loss is great and hard to bear*

*Like my childhood it seems to me*

*You would be forever there*

*But reality has weakened you*

*So like a child you flee*

*No earthbound mortal can*

*Constrain you -Go Ann -run to heavenly portals where you once more can be free*

*Go with God from whence you came*

*Let me cope with all you could not bear*

*But remember how I loved your foolish fancies*

*Remember all the years you dwelt with me*

*And if, what we believed was so – is so–*

*Come back and dwell with me when I go there.*

## DEAR GOD

*I hear a voice from some far distant realm,*

*But as a voice, from angry seas is a distant–*

*Cannot be – understood, by the salorr at the helm–*

*So it is with me!*

*I only know, I must hold fast–*

*Against the angry tides, the lashing wind, and waves,*

*And do the best I can, with every ounce of strength – to try.–*

*Tho fearful – to my very depth of being,*

*To look, to act, to be, in spite of me,*

*Somehow brave!*

*Even knowing, there are hidden shoals,*

*That keep me from desired goals,*

*Sometimes running with the tide,*

*Seeking harbor safe, in which to hide,*

*Until the storm abates !*

*Than in anger, heading straight into the wind–*

*" In defiance!*

*Desperate – to find the land, beyond Elysian gates;*

*But oh, the night is long,*

*Endless, weary hours, till the break of dawn,*

*And upon my cheeks, salt spray – or tears?,*

*I cannot tell;*

*For salt spray lashed, while salt tears fell !*

*I hurt, I weary, I straining for a single gleam of light;*

*To herald the break of a bright new day–*

*To dispel this endless night!*

## DEAR MR. MORGENSTEIN

*Hello Mr. Morgenstein*

*Isn't this a lovely day*

*The birds are singing*

*The sun is shining*

*What is that you say?*

*You're not feeling very well*

*The government has gone to hell*

*No one loves you – can that be so?*

*And money's running very low*

*Ah poor Mr. Morgenstein*

*What's happened to your youthful dreams*

*What's happened to the faith you had*

*That nothing ever could stay bad*

*That everything would turn out right*

*If you would just believe and fight*

*To make the world a better place*

*And bring a smile to just one face*

*You know what you believed was so*

*How could you have let it go?*

*Can't you see what you have lost*

*Or do you ever count the cost?*

*Of giving up on God and man*

*And the great eternal plan*

*Ah dear Mr. Morgenstein*

*You're making me feel sad*

*To know how much you're aching*

*And that you're feeling bad*

*See there? I care about you*

And many more do too

But what you give you shall receive

So it is up to you

Dear

Mr.

Morgenstein!


## DEARLY BELOVED

Rainbow hues – varied views

Stormy days and bright endless talk

And silence, tranquility and fright.

Rainbow hues – opposing views – the endless circle turns

And caught within the maelstrom the gentle person yearns.

They ask a million questions

About the goal she seeks

Then in the din of voices

Never hears her when she speaks.

They disagree about her, each one sure how she should live.

The wave of thunderous voices drowns out the LOVE she
gives.

And carries her on tides of passion to lonely barren shores.

And tho they try, it's all in vain to reach her anymore.

For a moment they are silent when they sense what they
have done

*But not for long for soon they find <u>another</u> gentle one.*

*They begin again for maybe*

*They will succeed this time*

*And so the circle turns again, no reason and no rhyme*

*Round and round, round and round the vicious circle turns*

*And caught within the maelstrom*

*The gentle person yearns.*

## DEJA VU

*The cold harsh rain falls like whiplash from the April sky,*

*While overhead a single loon in flight lets out this anguished cry*

*Unaware that on the dreary sodden earth below,*

*In spite of all, tiny fragrant snow drops dare to grow*

*Like Deja Vu, a memory from much gentler times*

*Peeks from childhoods' corridors and fills the woman's mind*

*As «then»–she kneels, cold–alone–*

*«As then»–»Again»–the tiny blooms «promise»–*

*God is There !*

*And suddenly–tho nothing's changed–a small light starts to grow*

*In form, much like a snowdrop–as peace begins to flow,*

*She lifts her head, as tears flow softly mixing with the rain*

*And whispers—Thank you! For your love back then and*
*«now» again!*

# DESPAIR

*The World Of Monetary Gain, Of Rape And Lust*
*Of Greed And Pain*
*Closed In, Until I Felt—That It Would Smother Me*
*So—As Long Ago—I Fled To Where I Felt My Spirit Could Be*
*Free!*
*A Small Secluded Forest Glen—Beside A Lake—Where Men*
*Of Self Importance Never Go*
*Searching For Tranquility—The Me—I Used To Know!*
*But As I Slowly Walked, I Sensed A Difference There*
*Then Within My Soul I Wept*
*Filled With Deep Despair*
*For The Lovely Trees Of Long Ago—The Stately Trees I Used*
*To Know*
*Were Twisted—Dead Or Dying—With Branches Hanging Low*
*Diseased And Yet—Still Trying To Live—And Somehow, Grow*
*I Stood Transfixed, I Seemed To Mix With Their Reality*
*The Fear The Pain The Horror Of Every Single Tree*
*Became My Own As Their Life Forces*
*Very Nearly Spent—Screamed In Protest At Their Fate*
*And Wailed Their Sad Lament*

*While Round Their Roots, The Lake Of Acid Lapped*

*Seeming Not To Know–It's Waters Now Were Deadly*

*That Nothing More Would Grow*

*It Followed Natures Pattern Blindly With No Mind*

*As It Had In Eons Past Thru The Mists Of Time*

*Unaware That Now–It Had No Life To Give*

*Polluted By The Hand Of Man–No Life Within It Lived*

*Then A Cold Wind Stung Me, Chilling Thru And Thru*

*The Day Was Old–And I Was Cold–And Nothing I Could Do*

*Could Restore The Beauty That I Had Known And Lost*

*I Had Not Cared When It Was There*

*Enough To Count The Cost*

*Of Letting Others Like Me–Do As They Damn Well Pleased*

*Without A Fight To Stop Them*

*To Save Our Lakes And Trees*

*We Have To Care! If They're Not There*

*What Then, Will We Do?*

*The End Of Nature Spells The End Of All*

*The End Of Me–Of You*

# THE DIFFERENCE IS DISCERNABLE

*You came into my life and you loved me*

*The sun shone so brightly on that day*

*I felt warm, protected, and wanted,*

*And longed for this feeling to stay*

*For your loving was good, like the Scriptures*

*And all that was fine was in you—*

*You taught me the <u>meaning</u> of love dear,*

*And in turn I learned how to love too!*

*Then <u>you</u> came into my life and <u>you</u> loved me*

*And my heart was burdened with pain,*

*The way that <u>you</u> loved me was heavy*

*And all sunshine became cold, drenching rain,*

*No comfort, no hope did you offer*

*No protection! Just demands of my soul!*

*And slowly all hope died of starvation*

*The world stopped, and just became old*

## DIFFERENT

*I awakened from a dream – in which I heard the banshee scream*

*Twas the middle of the night—*

*No one was there – to comfort me – or to hold me tight—*

*All the world was resting – as they well should be—*

*But there is neither rest – nor peace – for the likes of me*

*Tormented soul – awakened – by a troubled dream*

*Tormented soul – awaiting – a new day's troubled scene—*

*Filled with great forebodings – knowing I must face—*

*All it means in life or dreams – in the human race–*

*To be a "different" spirit – one not understood–*

*Discerned by some – as evil – by others labeled – "Good"*

*"Both" – become a burden – that I cannot bear–*

*And all I am – so complex – I find I cannot share–*

*What it means to walk the night – lonely and alone!*

*What it's like to live each day – strictly on my own!*

## DON'T INVOLVE YOUR HEART

*You're Wonderful, I love You*

*You make my body sing!*

*But - Tho I care about you-*

*This is - "A nowhere" - Thing!*

*It's true! You gave fair warning From the very start-*

*Enjoy the moment - but Remember!*

*- Don't involve your Heart!*

*I wanted to be with you-*

*And like a little fool-*

*I thought that I could live-*

*According to - "Your Rules!"*

*But darlin - "Just Can't do it!"*

*So guess I'll travel on!-*

*Searching for the Ultimate-*

*"Love's Eternal Song!"*

Somehow I know - it can't be so

But what Shall be - shall be

I must live - and I must give

Or know futility! But either way I cannot dwell

"Within" this - "No Man's Land!"

That's been - "The Story of my Life"-

And So - -0 I seek - "The Hand!"

Of one who knows - the Loneliness-

The sheer futility, of needs unanswered,

"Love" - "UNfulfilled"

"Someone" Just Like Me!

## THE DREAMER

It seems each night when ere I lie

Another one I can't deny

Replaces me and walks where I

Would never dare to go

Who is this person saying "I"

Meaning me, meaning she,

And how much does she know?

Why does she walk in winter

When summer fills the land?

Why does she leave this planet?

For some forgotten strand

Where Aliens exist, then vanish in the mist,

Where mountains rise to touch the skies,

And the Iron grip

Of fear, turns into rainbows

Tears turn into smiles

Days become but moments

A corner into miles

She makes no sense when I awake

So I dismiss her then

But every night when ere I lie

She comes to life again

For her there are no rules

No boundaries, no time

No concerns or caring–for this life of mine

But then I think, why should she?

When she's the best of me

Daring anything

In order to be free!

She walks the very universe,

Back and forth thru time

Protected only by her faith

In a force divine

That lets her taste the bitter cost

The loneliness, the fear, the loss,

*Then takes away the bitter cup*

*Empties it–and fills it up*

*With nectar sweet as wine*

*Ambrosia, that fills her soul*

*With a love divine*

*Either way, it does not matter*

*Love–or utter waste*

*She longs to know completeness*

*So greedily she tastes*

*Until the cup is empty–and sometimes so is she,*

*But she embraces all that comes*

*Whatever it may be*

*She risks it all–because the call*

*To utter ecstasy*

*From which she was abolished so very long ago*

*Calls her back from what she is–to what she used to know,*

*And someday I shall cease to be–no more body*

*No more me! Then she will be! Yes she will be!*

*To guide us then–to Ecstasy!*

*Where we have always longed to be!*

## DUMPED

*You said goodbye and I didn't cry*

*But my world ended yesterday*

*I couldn't believe it I wanted to die*

*As I watched you walk away*

*Do you know how much I love you*

*Don't you even care*

*That the pain inside when I hear your name*

*Is more than I can bear?*

*I keep hearing your laugh, seeing your face*

*So gay, so wonderfully free,*

*I know you will love Oh God above*

*If only it could have been me.*

## EXISTING

*I walked alone for a thousand years*

*I've been alone in a valley of tears*

*I am alone–tho I am wed*

*And I am living tho I am dead*

*Nobody hears me or answers my prayer*

*Thousands of people and nobody there*

*Why am I here? I just don't know*

*I guess I exist just because it is so*

*If I could find joy what a life it would be*

*But instead I mark time until I am free*

# FAITH RESTORED

*She Spoke Of All The Wondrous Years*

*And As She Spoke The Gentle Tears*

*Flowed Softly Down Her Cheeks*

*Then She Whispered "All Is Gone"*

*"I'm Not Sure I Can Go On".*

*Thru All This Pain And Fear!*

*For There Is Nothing Left For Me*

*All That Was–That Used To Be*

*Except For Me–Had Died!*

*No! I Said–It Is Not Dead*

*Thru You! It Is Alive!*

*There Are Wonders I Have Known*

*But They Are Mine And Mine Alone*

*Unless I Choose To Share*

*As You Have Chosen So To Do*

*Hoping I Might Care*

*And I Do! For Thru You–I Have Come To See*

*That Only Things That Touch The Soul*

*Shall Live In Memory!*

*Like Shadow Or Like Sunlight*

*Those Who Enter In*

*Can Lead Us On A Rainbow Path*

*Or Lead Us Into Sin*

*But Always We'll Remember*

*Just How It Used To Be*

*For Good Or Bad It All Resides*

*Within Our Memory!*

*Each One A Little Different*

*Yet Very Much The Same*

*Inclined Thru Love To Linger*

*Or, To Run Because Of Pain*

*But You Are Lucky! Don't You Know?*

*For If You Had You're Way You'd Go*

*Back Thru Time And Space*

*Where Once You Knew Such Joy And Love*

*That Now You Cannot Face*

*The Lack Of It*

*But Do Not Cry, Rejoice! Do Not Despair*

*For Many Do Not Know This Place*

*They Never Have Been There!*

*You Were Blessed–With Happiness*

*That Made You What You Are*

*While Others Live Within A Hell,*

*You Dwell Among The Stars!*

# FANTASY

*Within my soul I see the realms beyond man's comprehension–*

*Within my mind I see – what is known as fantasy, in limitless dimension–*

*"Within" lives beauty, eternity – and God!*

*The source of "All!"*

*"Within" from eons past my spirit heeds the call*

*But I am caught within a form – struggling since birth–*

*To reconcile "ethereal" with "facts" of planet Earth*

*There is no reconciliation! So, why, then, do I try?*

*Too weary from the effort – I cannot even cry–*

*Yet still! "Within" in spite of all, I hear the echoes of that call–*

*That speaks of ancient things – I sense the presence*

*Feel a touch – like gentle – angels' wings–*

*Then once again I see a light from some far distant land*

*And reach towards it humbly – with a mortal hand*

*Knowing it's beyond my grasp – a fleeting glimpse that cannot last–*

*It's not yet meant for me–*

*But someday I shall know the love that lives eternally!*

*And I shall dwell – were once I dwelt before this dream called life!*

*And I shall close the book I read*

*Of pain, despair, and strife–*

*Happy it was just a dream and not reality–*

*Glad to be home – with those I love – and feel their love for me!*

## FANTASY GIRL

*In the land of memory- once upon a time*

*Dwelt a maid called Fantasy- very good at mime*

*No one knew from whence she came or what she really thought*

*Each time they tried – she'd hide in mime*

*So she would not get caught*

*Being what "she really was" for she thought – you see!*

*They would laugh- so she determined*

*"Never – to – BE ME!"*

*Instead she noted each small thing*

*They would say or do*

*And they believed her when she said*

*I'm not me! I'm you!*

*For she would mime them perfectly*

*(At least as they would like to be)*

*But as the years went by – they did not come*

*As, once, they had – and she wondered why*

*She felt alone and frightened*

*What was she to do?*

*Could not remember who she was*

*Just you – and you – and you!*

*"Twas then she knew – she must leave*

*The land of memory*

*Where – once upon a time – she was known as Fantasy*

*She carried with her, only, what she could hold within her heart*

*Just a few delusions (with which she could not part)*

*She followed now the rugged path of "what I have to do"*

*Against the storm that howled – be them!*

*You never can be you*

*To late – to late – old lady – never can you be*

*Anyone at all – if you're not Fantasy!*

*The mountains of displeasure – you shall never climb*

*And even should you make it you will only find*

*Between what you have been and what you seek to be*

*An ocean treacherous and cold – called Reality!*

*Many times her spirit failed as doubt assailed her mind*

*Tempting her – do not try*

*Go back! Return! In time*

*And several times she turned*

*But could no longer find the way*

*So onward now in doubt she strived*

*Day by single day*

*Until at last, she came, to a cold and endless sea*

*The last and final test – cruel Reality!*

*Numb from the endless journey, trying*

*Still, she dove straight in*

*Then she began with all her will this*

*Final test to win*

*And this is where we leave – this maid called Fantasy*

*Swimmer in the sea of cruel Reality*

*The mists of time enshroud her*

*Now and forever more*

*Perhaps she will - or never will*

*Reach the distant shore*

*Of the land of warmth and love*

*Where she could truly be*

*"Proud" – no matter what that was*

*Just – in being – "ME!"*

## GIFT OF LOVE

*When we love, we send a message,*

*Warm and Sweet and True*

*To another life form,*

*That, then, responds to all we do.*

*Thru Love - all Wisdom came to be*

The guiding-guardian energy

That at its very core Retains in truth,

Each answer that we've been searching for.

But mostly we just <u>Say</u> we love

Then dutifully we do

What is expected

Right or wrong

To make our words come true.

Then Pridefully we strut and boast

Of what we've done or know

Convincing others, (or at least Ourselves)

That our love has made it so!

Why then? Sits the Loved one?

In a corner Bare!

With Breaking heart because of fear,

Alone! - With no one there?

I've been, and often am

In such a desperate place,

Then softly like a gentle hand

Thru time and fear and space

Comes a message of pure Love

Warm and Sweet and True

From another life form

that blesses all I do!

*Tis then in heartfelt Gratitude*

*My soul cries out to Thee*

*Thou Art of God*

*Who in His Love*

*Sets all His People Free.*

## THE GLORY SEEKERS

*Ah vain people – think you're better far than anyone you
know?*

*Prance and dance in clothing new – today*

*Rags tomorrow – But while the music plays*

*Put on your show!*

*Speak low back of upraised hand – filth and Slime*

*That robs the one you malign*

*And gains you nothing!*

*Climb your ladder of success step on all to gain the peak*

*Hoard the decaying things of earth*

*And when you come to the barren lonely place known as the
summit – Weep!*

*No where else to go, and none to care!*

*For who is there – that should?*

*The hurt- warped desperate souls you used to get you there?*

*See you now! Clothed in all the finest mankind can provide*

*Possessed with possessions yet precarious the Summit*

*No where there to hide them*

*The Spotlight shines and greedy eyes behold the glitter*

*Longing – Clawing for the place <u>you</u> hold*

*Then the show is over – pulled into the darkness – Death!*

*All is gone, except one single thing*

*The Soul!*

*But so weak – so weak, from lack of nourishment*

*It struggles to be free – to rise, too late beholds*

*The beauty of love and truth – melts and writhes*

*In torment!*


## GOLDEN BELLS

*Heaven they say is Beautiful*

*Wondrous to Behold*

*A place of warmth and Happiness*

*With streets made of purest gold*

*Golden voices rang in chorus*

*Proclaiming Jesus' Birth*

*Gold, Frankincense and Myrrh*

*Were brought by wise men of this "Earth"*

*The greatest love and friendships*

*Are held as valuable as gold*

*And of purest tones of Christmas comes*

*From Golden bells we're told*

*So sweetie when you feel that nothing is worthwhile*

*Ring this little golden Bell*

*And it will make you smile*

*Then when you smile you'll have given all your friends a lift*

*And if they love you truly*

*This will be your greatest gift*

*For as you give so you'll receive*

*And soon all will be well*

*This is the hope and love we send*

*With this tiny Golden Bell*

## GOOD GUYS

*I'd like to think the Good Guys always win*

*But very seldom is it true–mostly I've watched all of you*

*The Bad Guys win hands down*

*The Good Guys? They become the fools*

*The losers, perhaps clowns*

*Yeah! Bad Guys–I mean all of you*

*You're most adept at what you do*

*And you do it very well*

*Destroying all that's fine and good*

*Like raging hounds of hell!*

*And in this evil holocaust*

*So many innocents are lost, and who's there to care?*

Like screams from Auschwitz went unheard

For there were few who dared

To speak the truth—admit the truth

For this just could not be

So said the ones with hearts of stone

Its all a Fallacy!

So we believed and were deceived

While millions suffered—died

Heeding not the voice of truth

They're being crucified!

It wasn't you—it wasn't me

Why then should we care?

What could we do? If it were true!

We weren't even there!

But why the Hell were we not there?

When we were needed so?

Why the lack of courage to buck the status quo?

Are we better than the Bad Guys?

Somehow I think—we're not!

Without the courage to defy

We are a sorry lot!

Bible thumpers giving way—life by life

Day by Day

To those with stronger will

Shirley Ann Wood

# THE GREATEST GIFT

*The world is full of Wonder*

*But honey, it took you-*

*To bring it all together,*

*By the things you say and do-*

*To make me know - really know-*

*deep within my heart*

*That I could share that wonder-*

*And of it, be a part !*

*Once I was blind, but now I see-*

*All that God has given me*

*And never more will I-*

*Take for granted - peace of mind,*

*Or a clear blue sky !*

*A Hug, a wink, a friendly smile,*

*Softly falling rain - Love extended-*

*Or with held, because of someone's pain*

*A cozy blanket, falling snow-*

*I could go on and on*

*With wonder after wonder-*

*The Day ! The Night ! The Dawn!*

*Each holding their own special gifts,*

*Showered from above*

*And "Life" the greatest Gift of all –*

*When lived*

*with Joy and Love!*

## GREEN

*The colour green I know must be*

*The favorite colour of He*

*That created the earth*

*For every tree*

*And field as far as can be seen*

*Wears a lovely mantle of*

*Many shades of green*

*And then of course I knew too*

*God must love the colour blue*

*For the ocean and the sky*

*And every river running by*

*Bluebells bobbing in the breeze*

*Bluebirds singing in the trees*

*Robins' eggs, and berries too*

*Proclaim His love for shades of blue.*

*Then of course the colour brown*

*Everywhere you look it's found.*

*Sparrows, nightingales and wrens*

*Fresh turned earth and*

*Men of many nations*

*Yes, you have but to look around to know*

*How much God loves brown.*

*At least that's how it seems to me*

*That these four colours are the ones that He, loves best*

*Yet who can say – for sure, when all the rest*

*Are far more beautiful too than any words convey*

*Perhaps each one's His favourite in its own wondrous way!*

*Yet it wouldn't seem quite right*

*Not to mention yet another*

*The total lack of any colour*

*Which we know as white*

*God chose this as another symbol of His love*

*The stars that shine, the gentle cooing dove*

*The frost that patterns every window pane*

*The clouds, the snow*

*The gently falling rain.*

## GROWING UP

*I've been told this by everyone I know,*

*But stop–and remember if you can–*

*The world of a child not the world of a man*

*Wasn't it a lovely place?*

*And wasn't there kindness in every face?*

*So much to do, and places to go–*

*But wait—ah yes, I know—*

*A child has only faith and trust,*

*He hasn't yet learned to deceive and distrust*

*Hasn't learned that to get things these rules are a must*

*And my life is changed and somehow, tho I've tried,*

*I can't regain those dreams that burned like a living flame.*

*For others will not have it so,*

*I must get ahead you know*

*I must be quick and good at scheming*

*And never mind that childish dreaming*

*They haven't lived, they don't yet know*

*That good things don't come from wishing it so.*

## GUIDANCE

*I Have Lived A Rich Full Life*

*The End I Won't Regret*

*For Children It's Inevitable*

*Birth And Life, Then Death.*

*I Would Not Have You Cry For Me*

*For This Truth I Have Learned*

*Tears Are Just A Waste Of Time*

*And Time Must Not Be Spurned.*

*But We Use Each Moment Carefully*

*Each Hour, Every Day*

*Learn To Love Humanity*

*Be Humble When You Pray.*

*Look At The Beauty Of The Stars*

*Feel The Warmth Of The Sun*

*And Fill Your Lives With Laughter*

*Work Hard, Have Faith, Have Fun.*

*Dream Dreams Of The Impossible*

*Then Work To Make Them So*

*No Goal's Too High*

*And With God's Help*

*You'll Reach You're Goals I Know!*

*Cry Only In Compassion*

*Hold Out A Helping Hand*

*And When You Choose Your Life Mate*

*Be It A Woman Or A Man*

*Look For A Sense Of Humor*

*Avoid The One Who's Stern*

*For There Will Be Some Trying Times*

*In Which You'll Have To Turn*

*To Another For Reassurance.*

*My Children I Pray That You*

*Will Choose A Life Mate Carefully And Well*

*For One Who Never Smiles Or Bends*

*Can Make Your Life A Hell!*

*And Then Your Laughter Would Die In Your Heart*

*And You Would Bitter Be*

*Remember What I've Told You*

*For Gloom Is Slavery!*

## HAPPY BIRTHDAY

*Happy Birthday, Child Of My Youth*

*Sweet Promise Of All That Would Be*

*Part Of My Soul, My Flesh And My Heart*

*So Tiny–So Precious–To Me!*

*First Born Of Many A Dream*

*I Hoped And I Prayed Would Come True*

*Began The Eighth Of November*

*The First Time I Ever Met You.*

*I Nestled You Close, My Life You Beguiled*

*Learning Together–Child Teaching Child*

*Growing Together Down Through The Years*

*In Love And Compassion, Laughter And Tears.*

*Moment By Moment I Watched You Grow*

*And Moment By Moment The Years Seemed To Go*

*Flowing Like Water To Some Distant Land*

*Transporting The Babe–Evolving The Man.*

*But Still, On This Day, I Remember And Smile*

*For When I Remember, "Just For A While"*

*I Am A Young Mother, In My Reverie,*

*And Thoughts Of You, Always, So Special To Me*

*Are Gentle And Strong–Much Like My Son*

*And Though We Grow Older, We'll Always Be Young.*

*The Eighth Of November, Where We Used To Be*

*The Day God Decided To Send You Go Me*

*And Though We Must Dwell So Far Apart,*

*You Always Will Be "As Close As My Heart".*

## HAPPY BIRTHDAY HONEY

*On your birthday I remember*

*All the passing years*

*Funny things, sunny things, magic,*

*Laughter, tears,*

*I remember times you needed me*

*And times I needed you–*

*How together we were stronger*

*In what we had to do.*

*But mostly I remember*

*The times I held you tight*

*Knowing that thru love and hope*

*All things would work out right*

*And so they did, and so they do*

*'Cause you love me and I love you*

*So Happy Birthday Honey*

*What more can I say?*

*Except perhaps God Bless you*

*On this! Your Special Day!*

## HAPPY BIRTHDAY KAREN

*May you have dreams in your mind – you can always share*

*Hope in your heart to always care*

*And someone with you – always there*

*To fill your life with love*

*May your days be sweet*

*And rich – and good*

*Unfolding before you as they should*

*Guided by God above*

*All this and more I wish for you*

*On this – your special day*

*For you were born*

*To seek – to find*

*Your own, your special way*

*I held you and I loved you*

*At the moment of your birth*

*Believe me – when I tell you*

*Of the value, of the worth*

*Of all you are, and all you do*

*Each day on planet earth!*

*So – Happy Birthday Honey*

*May God bless you on this day*

*And walk beside you always*

## HAPPY ENDINGS

*As a child, how I loved – happy endings – surmised they always should be*

*No matter how bad the beginnings – there would be happy endings for me*

*I lived in a world that danced in my mind – a beautiful world – gentle and kind–*

*Filled with God's creatures – so varied – so free–*

*In my mind I was loved – as they were – by me–*

*I basked in the sunlight – danced in the rain–*

*Gazed in wonder, at frost, that formed, on the panes–*

*Picked violets, musky, with sweet morning dew–*

*All part of the world – that I once loved and knew*

*Each life form a burst of creation, and creation an unending spree–*

*Of colour, and music, and magic, and love that was showered on me–*

*And my Father – the God of creation! The source of <u>all</u> that could be!*

Was the one who held in the palm of His hand – happy
endings – always – for me!
So forgive me – if now – I grow quiet – recede–
From this <u>real</u> world, where unicorns, suffer – and bleed!
Where the children of darkness cause havoc and pain–
Where endings are bitter – time and again!

## HIDING PLACE

There is a place I often hide
A secret place so deep inside
A place where none can follow me
Where all the things that used to be
Make me feel I'm not alone
A gentle feeling of coming home
I long to stay but all too soon
I find I have to go
Out of my world, back to the world
Of pain and tears and woe
Reality that kills the dream
And all is just the way it seems,
But someday I will run and hide
And never have to come outside
Just follow all I know to be
Until I reach the one who's really me.

Shirley Ann Wood

# HIDING PLACES

*Hiding places in the mind*

*Where only one <u>can</u> live*

*Not shared by others of mankind*

*Will <u>this one</u> take? Or give?*

*No way to tell, what to do*

*Can I trust you? Or you? Or you?*

*I'd like to think you mean no harm,*

*For nestled here within my arms,*

*Is my whole world you see*

*How you think, affects <u>my</u> life–*

*And others just like me*

*We trust, we work, we hope, we pray,*

*Hearing every single day – of new atrocities*

*We cannot understand at all, how you (how <u>this</u>) can be!*

*For ones without compassion*

*Stink of decay and death*

*And they shall reap – what they shall sow–*

*Until there's nothing left*

*While those who <u>know</u> compassion*

*Watched by God above shall have*

*Everlasting life - Thru the power of love.*

*So I, and others like me, tho we have pain and fear–*

*Shall do the very best we can–*

*Knowing God is near!*

# THE HYPOCRITE

*Hello Lady! Got a dime? Said a ragged urchin of the street*

*No! Go away! Ugh*

*Filthy creature –*

*Go away I say - don't stand there looking like a jackass-*

*Then sneering - can you bray?*

*No but I can whistle*

*I do it all the time-*

*Or sing a song-I'll do that too if you'll*

*Gimme a dime*

*Stupid child just move away I have no dime for you*

*I have a meeting to attend-important things to do*

*And so she left and the urchin stood and scratched his tousled head-*

*Then to his brother turned, come on don't just stand there git to askin*

*Things is pretty rough for Ma since Dad got dead*

*The lady? Oh!*

*Her meeting was for welfare in the slums-*

*To help the little children*

*The underprivileged ones.*

# I AM

*"I Am"–It Has Been The Ancient Cry Of Man*

*The Statement Of His Being*

*I Cry–I Laugh–I Feel–I Think–I Love–*

*I Know!–I Am!*

*Born Alone–My Thoughts, My Own*

*And As I Think–I Live!*

*My Decision,–Mine Alone*

*If I Shall Take–Or Give!*

*My Mind–Unique!*

*None Can Enter, Only I Live There*

*To Feel The Depths, And Heights Of Passion*

*Fear, Love, Hope, Despair!*

*Tread Lightly Then–If You Would Mould Me,*

*Or Seek To Bend Me To Your Will*

*Tho Outwardly–I May Comply*

*My Soul Rebels*

*Retreats–And Stands*

*Observing You–Angry! Solemn! Still!*

*And Waits! Until The Time, It Once More Can Be Free!*

*As God Commanded!*

*I Must Think And Be–What I Must Be!*

*But I Have Such A Little Time To Accomplish What I Can,*

*For Soon I'll Die–As I Was Born,*

*Alone!*

*To Leave This World Of Man*

The Body That Has Harboured Me

Will Decay,–And Cease To Be!

Naked Now–I'll Stand Revealed!

All Deceptions Left On Earth

"No Lie" To Shield Me–Just A Clear Bright Light,

Of What I Am

Or Am Not

Worth!

Too Late Then For You To Help Me

So Please!

Help Me While You Can!

Don't Burden Me!

Let Me Be Free!

To Be

Just What I Am!!!


## I WISH

How I wish that I <u>could</u> be,

Instead of me!

A ray of sunlight

Bringing forth from earthly beds

All living Things!

Touching heads –

Of all the Children

*Great or small, in every land*

*Dancing on the many oceans*

*Playing on the Continents*

*Warming all, Exposed to me*

*Fulfilling God's great plan*

*No doubts, no heartaches would there be*

*If I were just a ray of sunlight*

*'Stead of me!*

*Ah, How I wish!*

*But it's not so!*

*Yet everyday – each place I go*

*I do have sense enough to know*

*That tho, there's anger, fear, and pain*

*Dark places filled with gloom and Rain*

*I would not visit them again*

*Unless it Just must be!*

*The beauty of a sunlit day*

*Appeals much more to me!*

*I love its dancing, laughing way*

*And seek its warmth with each new day*

*So all must be – as it must be*

*According to its destiny*

*And tho I long to change my place*

*I am of the Human Race*

Earthbound, I cannot change the laws

That bind and shackle me

Just Hope and pray on my last day

My Spirit be set free

So I may go where ere I wish


# THE IMAGE

Can't seem to live up, to this Image you have,

Of all you would like me to be

You'll have to decide—what you really want

This daydream—this Image—or me!

I've tried very hard, to change all I am

So you'd love me—The way I love you!

But I keep coming back

To the way that I am!

So, if what I am—just won't do!

Please, Remember

I tried—"cause I love you"

To become, what you'd like me to be!

Tho it's breaking my heart—"I cannot become"

This Image—who's nothing like me.

I'm just the one—who will always be there

No matter what you choose to do

"No Image, No daydream, Nobody on earth"

Could touch me the way that you do!

You're warm flesh and blood, "and I need you"

But each time I reach out

"You're not there!"

You keep searching to find

This one in your mind

The one who never would dare

To ruin this daydream, this Image you have

Of all you would like her to be

And perhaps–you will find her,

You'll be certain to know

If this Image is nothing like me!


## I'M HERE

Where is the light?

The end of night?

Within this lonely sphere!

Please answer me–

Please come to me–

I'm here!

Where are the dreams

That once I knew?

Where is the comfort?

Where are you?

*I'm here!*

*Can't you find me?*

*Don't you know?*

*That if you just don't care!*

*I'm here!*

*Why did you leave-*

*And where?*

*Where did you go?*

*Even tho I loved you so!*

*Please answer me*

*Please come to me*

*I'm here–*

*Just waiting – here!*

## LEECHES

*The Songs Have Ceased-*

*And All Around*

*The Sounds I've Always Feared-*

*Abound!*

*Sung By Those*

*Who Do Not Live*

*Except Thru Lives That Others Give*

*To Keep Them Strong And Fat And Well*

*Leeches From The Bowels Of Hell*

# LESS THAN ANGELS

*A little less than angels*

*We were created long ago*

*Cut off thru disobedience*

*Veiled by mists of time*

*We only guess how once we were*

*But can never really know*

*Still we can guess if we just look-*

*To see the best of humankind*

*That is if we don't kill them first*

*And if there Still is time*

# LIFE FORM

*I look in the mirror, and there, I see;*

*An ancient one looking back at me,*

*How was it that the years slipped by,*

*As I was still forming an infant's cry?*

*All the wisdom I thought was mine,*

*Is as nothing in the vastness of time,*

*Deeds long gone – once vital to me,*

*Are like dreams unfulfilled – they've just ceased to be,*

*Looking back, looking through, the tunnel of time,*

*This life, this existence, I've always called mine,*

*Becomes intermingled with others – so much–*

As in a kaleidoscope – I cannot keep touch–
With the single small piece – as it tumbles around,
Forming patterns of beauty, as somewhere a sound–
In the silence, evolves, (at first plaintively)
Becoming a lullaby, once sung to me,
One after another, like laughter and tears,
The music of life, down through the years,
Blend together to form one sweet harmony,
Proclaiming events once important to me,
I hear songs of my childhood, then love songs so sweet,
Songs of great bravery, set to the beat,
Of drums that once sounded the rhythms of war,
Sad songs that questioned, what it was all for,
The songs of rejoicing, weddings and birth,
Proclaiming the glory of heaven and earth,
Then silence! The cycle of life has gone round,
And one tiny seed, falls to the ground,
There it shall lay, neath the deep winter snow,
Till the spring – when once more it shall root – perhaps
grow–
Never giving a thought, that it once used to be,
A life form renewed, that used to be me!

Shirley Ann Wood

# LIMBO

*Strangely quiet and subdued*

*All emotions frozen held in check*

*By some foreboding bonds of black*

*The future cloud itself I cannot see*

*That past to clear beckoning me*

*Look back, look back*

*Ah but my soul rebels*

*Four in the past is all I wished for,*

*All my dreams and hopes gone wrong*

*My life I said sole legacy*

*A discordant invitation*

*Of a hoped for lovely song*

*Where to turn? What to trust*

*If only I could see*

*One answer, see one hope*

*But day by day he in ever*

*Shrinking circles round and round I go*

*Weary, said and frustrated*

*Not knowing where to turn,*

*Yet in my mind*

*The memory of you*

*I once had dreamed*

*And now I only yearn*

*To see sunlight dance once*

*More on silver water that*

*Quickly lapped the shore*

*To smell a wildflowers*

*Arranged in brilliant hues*

*Watch shadows dance,*

*See horses prance*

*Feel the gentle touch, see*

*Once more the quick warm smile*

*No again the one I still remember, you!*

*You, as you used to be,*

*Holding forth the promise*

*Of happiness contentment*

*Love with me.*

*Floodwaters stormy, petals*

*Crushed sunlight turned to tears*

*Sweet scents of yesterday*

*Turned acid through the years*

*And now I stand no longer*

*Me as long ago I used to be*

*And with the loss of all*

*I built my life upon*

*Bewildered, I move thru*

*Each day and then another*

*Until they all soon will be gone*

*Yet still I cannot break*

*These bonds of black*

*In spite of all my will–*

*Dare not look forward*

*Cannot go back*

*Alone – Silently – I cry – In limbo!*

## LIMELIGHT

*Baby – you say you won't listen*

*To what your Mama has to say*

*Well okay – but baby remember*

*If the whole worlds your stage*

*Then you're " life" is the play*

*Well some plays are good*

*And some plays are bad*

*Some plays are happy*

*While others are sad*

*And baby you won't take direction*

*You never would right from the start*

*If you don't give others a chance*

*You're headed for a broken heart*

*You can't have the limelight all of the time*

*There are others who must have their turn .*

# LITTLE SISTER

*Little Sister with skin so fair*

*And eyes of Midnight Blue*

*I hear the whisper of yesterdays*

*That tell of my love for you*

*Unalike–yet much alike*

*Beneath our form and face*

*Created then neath different stars*

*Yet Sisters in God's Grace*

*Down thru corridors of time*

*Of Endless centuries*

*It was destined we should meet*

*And share our destiny*

*So in this twinkling of an eye–*

*The time that we shall live,*

*I want to thank you for your love*

*As my love, to you, I give*

*For love is life and life is love*

*For God and one another*

*Bestowed on us before our birth*

*Nourished by our Mother*

*Born to be a single thread*

*In the tapestry of time*

*Yet woven close together*

*Our lives are intertwined*

*Unalike–yet much alike*

*So it was meant to be*

*The pattern calls for contrast*

*Me for you, and you for me.*

## LONELY

*I've walked along by the lonely sea*

*And heard the Seagulls cry*

*I've waited an eternity*

*As I gazed at the darkened sky*

*I've searched where the lights were bright*

*And peered at many faces*

*It seems I've walked a million miles*

*In a million different places,*

*Perhaps – I've said – or done – or thought*

*Some terrible sinful thing*

*I don't know what – or when or why*

*But my heart no longer sings.*

*So I pray with my lips and hope to retrieve*

*All that I had long ago,*

*But no answer I get – for one must believe*

*And my dreams are as cold as the snow*

*No God can be fooled – deceived or beguiled*

By the things we have to say.

He gives us life – and

Guides us to love

But sometimes we throw it away

And then we walk by the lonely sea

And search it seems for eternity

Never finding peace of mind

Ever lonely – 'Til the end of time.

## LOST RADIANCE

Tears that drown the laughter

Fears that hold you still

Afraid to move and somewhere

Deep inside a stifled cry

As the radiance that should have been your life

Flares, flickers, dims and dies

Now like an automaton

The days, the years seem long

Only in the depths of memory

A song - of youth!

And in the eyes the memory cries out with silent, pleading–

But who would look to see?

Lost radiance sheds no light and so only

A plain and unexciting mortal do they see

*Did I choose? Or was this life in some dark cavern selected*

*By a cunning mind for me?*

## LOVE UNTOLD

*I Call You "Friend" Cause You Want It That Way,*

*I Bite My Lip, So I'll Never Say–I Love You!*

*Each Time That We Meet–I Quickly Hide*

*All The Hurtin' And Lovin' Deep Down Inside,*

*"Just A Friend", Always There! Cause You Want It That*
*Way*

*But My Heart Whispers Softly, Don't Go Darling, Stay*

*Cause I Love You!*

*I Remember A Time When You Loved Me Too*

*All The Hopes And The Dreams, And The Sweet Feel Of You*

*Fills My Heart With Such Pain, That It Breaks It In Two*

*Cause I Love You!*

*Now There Is Another Who Calls You Her Own,*

*While I'm Just A Friend, Who Makes It Alone*

*Alone Cause You Touched Me, In Your Special Way*

*So Deeply It Seems, I Can't Seem To Say–To Another*

*I Love You*

# LOVE'S RESTORATION

*Go Gently With Me Now Sweet Love*

*Kiss Me Tenderly*

*Enfold Me In Your Warm Embrace,*

*Whisper Soft To Me*

*Heal My Pain With Words Of Love*

*Consume Me Not With Fire*

*Restore This Broken Heart Of Mine*

*With Balm Of Sweet Desire*

*Rock Me Gently, Let Me Feel*

*The Beating Of Your Heart*

*And Drink My Fill Of Your Sweet Lips*

*Stay Now! Do Not Depart!*

*With Tender Eyes–Reach Deep Inside*

*And Touch The Soul Of Me*

*Coax It Forth From Where It Hides*

*Then Bid It To Be Free*

*That It Might Laugh And Dance Once More*

*As Once It Did–And Then*

*I Shall Be–The Soul Of Me*

*Restored–In Love–Again!*

## MADAM

*A simple thank you just won't do–*
*There's so much more I wish for you!*
*I would give you lovely days*
*With sunshine playing hide and seek,*
*Soft gentle rain, the song of birds*
*And flowers blooming 'round your feet.*
*Exotic scents from far off lands,*
*The tender touch of loving hands.*
*The happiest of lives to live–*
*But these things only God can give,*
*So I shall say a little prayer*
*Each time I think of you*
*That Heaven grant you all these things*
*And bless each thing you do!*

## THE MAJIC KEY

*I have no wisdom like the love*
*That burns as bright as flame*
*I have no love so tender*
*As the mere sound of his name*
*For let his name be spoken*
*And memories unwind*
*Like a lovely golden thread*

*Back thru space and time*

*And there he stands before me*

*I can feel his presence near*

*Hear his laugh, feel his love*

*See his Face so dear*

*See him bend to tie my shoe*

*Or stoop to take my hand*

*See him stride along the beach*

*Barefoot in the sand*

*So many things he taught me*

*Like why stars shine at night*

*So many things he showed me*

*Like seagulls taking flight*

*But how can words describe*

*The events of many years*

*How can words convey*

*The laughter and the tears*

*For as a simple painting*

*Only imitates the land*

*Words can only tell of*

*Not let you know the man*

*For there is just one like him*

*No two are born the same*

*And that is why each time*

*I hear someone speak his name*

*The love that is within my heart*

*Becomes the magic key*

*That opens up the door of time*

*On years of memory*

*So fashion well the key of love*

*And with it never part*

*For it is yours and yours alone*

*To hold within your heart*

## MAGIC MOMENT

*There was a magic moment*

*It seems so long ago*

*You touched my hand, my heart, my soul*

*Twas then I loved you so*

*You took me from the darkness*

*Of my deep despair*

*And all the world was rainbow wrapped*

*Because my love – you cared!*

*I was so happy for a while*

*The sight of you – your wondrous smile*

*Made life a fantasy*

*One I'd never dreamed existed – or could even be*

*So for a single moment – in all the time I've lived*

*I felt the joy of love received*

*As I joyously did give.*

## THE MAGIC MOMENT

*The day we met – down deep inside*

*Where one else could see*

*I discerned all that you were*

*And what you were – was right for me!*

*You'd kept it hidden thru the years*

*Surrounded by your silent tears*

*Held fast – by mental chains*

*Never more to be revealed – for fear of loss and pain*

*And yet like some neglected child*

*Hoping to be found – beguiled*

*It reached in trust – to – me!*

*Wrapped in my love – it ventured forth*

*"Soon" – It would be free*

*In caring – I was cared for*

*And your love - did dispel*

*The bonds of pain that held my heart*

*Releasing it from Hell*

*So for a while the sun shone bright*

*Magic stars lit every night*

*And every wish came true*

"Just because" you loved and cared

As I did, Love, for you!

We'd found what we'd been searching for

Hoped it would last – forever more

But it only could survive

If we had cared enough – thru faith

To keep this love alive

But we did not care enough

To treat what we were well

So they retreat – alone again

Back to their <u>single</u> Hells!

## MALIGNED

I Have Been Maligned!

Whether By Accident Or Design

Makes No Difference

As I Cower, Not Understanding

Licking My Wounds!

Puzzled, Hurt, I Had Offered Love

Frolicked Happily Like A Puppy

Never Noticing The Shadow From Above

And Then The Blows–But Why?

I Expected Only The Best Of My Fellow Kind

Now I Distrust, Fear And Caution

Fills My Mind.

# THE MAN OF SAMIRKAND

Behold the Man of Samirkand

Robed in Linen White

Beyond in silence stands the

Black Eternal Night

Pale Gold the countenance

With dark eyes almond shaped

Belied in mystery, holding knowledge,

- Kept from me-

He bows three times - first to the left - then forward to the right

He raises his hands above his head

And brilliant Rainbow hues

Spring from the ground and all around

The night is bright with Reds and golds and Blues

He speaks with voice unreal

And tho I do not understand his words

Great emotion do I feel

"Enter the colours". "Enter the colours"

His voice a soft command

Then vanishes to the sound of tinkling silver Bells

This Man of Samirkand !

Shirley Ann Wood

# MAYBE SO, MAYBE NOT

*Maybe so and maybe not*

*That once I was and I forgot*

*That once I was – what used to be*

*Did that affect – what now is me?*

*Or cannot I, now realize*

*So I surmise and fantasize*

*That once within the human race*

*I fulfilled a time and space*

*Wherein my life had meaning*

*That lends its grace on me*

*Within this life so full of strife*

*I will it not. To be!*

*Yet still I live and still I give*

*All there is of me*

*Hoping that what I believe*

*Was not some fantasy*

*But real – within some other time*

*Paying for this life of mine*

*Amending my mistakes*

*Living then in penance for*

*This life I live – a*

*Living human waste*

*For I know that I was destined*

*To be of stature tall*

94

Yet here I stand

Of no account – weak and frail and small

Searching for one moment

That supercedes it all

In which I feel that I should be

Beautiful and tall

I long to write all that I am

Within this heart of me

To heal the heart that's burdened

And set their spirit free

But how can I – reach to the sky?

When reaching brings such pain?

So I recede – I run and hide

To never reach again

But in receding I must pay

The offering of tears

To offset what I became

Throughout these many years

A soul that should have been a light

Not one encompassed by the night

## MERRY CHRISTMAS

It's Christmas time again–

And for too short a while

*Hostilities within the heart.*

*Cease, or at the very least, abate–*

*As we rejoice – and smile–*

*We decorate with wreath and Holly,*

*Purchase gifts of worth or folly*

*Trim our trees, wrap our gifts,*

*Rushing here and there*

*Baking, sewing, painting, cleaning–*

*Everything with utmost care*

*Hoping there will be enough–*

*Time and money too–*

*To cover all the many things that we have yet to do–*

*Like children, we want more! Then more!*

*Rushing now from store to store*

*Have we forgotten anything?*

*How will the weather be?*

*Did I buy enough for them?*

*So they won't outdo me?*

*Then suddenly the day has come*

*Merry Christmas everyone*

*Table set with food galore,*

*While in a corner on the floor,*

*Beneath the ribbons, tags and wrap,*

*Has fallen a figure from where it sat–*

*On a table low,*

*No one sees that it is missing–*

*In their glow – of satisfaction–*

*Hugging, laughing, kissing–*

*And if they chanced to notice–*

*How much would it matter?*

*As they idly replaced, midst the jovial chatter–*

*The tiniest piece of the Crèche–*

*To its rightful place–*

*The" Centre" of a decoration–*

*To remind us of God's grace!*

*Perhaps tho, it would matter, after all!*

*That the missing babe, that happened to fall–*

*The symbol of love, the symbol of joy,*

*The birth of God in a new baby boy*

*Would touch the heart in the heart of December–*

*And all would take pause, give thanks and remember–*

*That the greatest gift we ever could give–*

*Is to care, and take care, each day that we live*

*Of ourselves, of all others,*

*Who through Jesus the Christ–*

*Are all sisters and brothers*

*Simple? Yes! But, No!*

*But if it could happen, if it were so.*

*Then would all destruction cease,*

*And we could rejoice*

*In a new world of peace!*

## MISGUIDED

*God breathed the breath of life into mortal man*

*From His breath of purest love, the immortal soul began*

*For love was the beginning of the way things ought to be*

*Abusing love–misusing love–changed our destiny!*

*No longer fit for Eden–*

*By our free will we dwell*

*–Always seeking what we lost*

*Always fearing Hell!*

*And tho we seek–we give*

*Not love*

*One unto the other, instead like Cain*

*In anger–we kill our God–*

*Our brother!*

*And even those who realize–*

*All of this is so*

*Cannot change in any way*

*This evil–"status quo"*

*For as surely as there is a Cain*

*Able then must die!*

*If there's no love,*

*I cannot live–let Able then,*

*Be I!*

*For I am nothing Lord without thee,*

*Please ease this fear and pain–*

*I'd rather die like Able–*

*Than live and be like Cain.*

## MISSING INGREDIENT

*There are no rainbows anymore*

*No silver bells from distant shores*

*No creatures beautiful and wild*

*No unique, celestial child*

*No man of Samirkand to guide*

*No fantasy in which to hide*

*No place to go – No place to stay*

*Since the magic went away!*

*All that's left – is time! And tears!*

*Days and nights! – Months and years!*

*How many – matters not, to me – for now!*

*They're all the same – you see*

*The artist's brush that was my soul*

*Painting pictures of my goals*

*In colours bright as fire*

*Formed in imagination – shaded by desires*

*Slowly turned to shades of grey*

*As all the colours spilled away*

## MISTS OF TIME

*Soft Mists in –*

*Shafts of sunlight drips in ribbons thru the trees*

*Plays along a wooded path*

*And melts into a pond of liquid gold*

*It twinkles coquettishly at a soft warm summer breeze*

*And laps at violets on the bank*

*Their roots to tenderly enfold*

*Then lovingly moves thru narrow banks and races lightly over pebbles*

*While, gaining momentum*

*Whirls a stump – crashes hard against it banks then leaps in sheer delight over a precipice*

*Becomes a silver curtain or twisting*

*Changing wall with rainbow colours and thunderous sound*

*A wonderful waterfall*

*Now exhausted rests a moment*

*Then moves on – a majestic – mighty river*

*Flowing thru the land*

*Until its final goal is reached*

*And it joins the water's salt that*

*Caress the sun- bleached sand*

*The ocean, Cradle of Life*

*From which the Mists –*

*And Mists of Time began.*

## MOTHER

*Mother what a world of Warmth and understanding that
single word implies*

*Like Home and God and Country always there dependable
and warm a refugee from the Storm*

*But implication alone does not mean it's so*

*For as the world cries God, God, unto the very skies*

*So do some call silently Mother, Mother see my pain
comfort me*

*for if you who gave me birth love me not*

*My very soul Will be desolate and all that I attempt will
come to naught*

*For as some build their houses on solid rock*

*For some there is no foundation except the one that's built
on sand,*

*Look about you See the trembling lives then look once more
See the desperate reaching hands*

*Reaching for a dream, a belief, not finding anything to grasp,*

*Arms flailing aimlessly for lack of one to understand*

*Lives lived Joylessly, with hope that dies and is reborn to die a thousand times*

*Until at last the body that has struggled against all odds sinks slowly in the engulfing sand*

*Then at last, a stillness, and somewhere*

*God looks with compassion and nods to one so loving, understanding*

*go and bring me the soul to me hold it by the hand, take it from the sand then smiling*

*Jesus says learn again, feel again all that you have needed, you will find*

*This my Mother, the example the best of Humankind*

*Mary ever loving tried to show all who would heed her example*

*how to be a mother, for even tho the Path I chose brought her pain*

*She never interfered just believed and loved and was always there*

*tending to every hurt again and yet again.*

*Now she will heal your wounds my sister and my brother-*

*There are so many of you yet we have had some help by those*

*Who try to emulate her and as best they can care more for the*

*Souls entrusted to them than for their own desires,*

*for these have lit the lives of others with Love that finally*

*became the brightest lights you see in Heaven*

*Pure and clean like incandescent Wires*


## A MOTHER'S THOUGHTS

*Man took a twig and planted it deep*

*And it grew to be a tree*

*Then he cut it down my baby to make a cradle for thee*

*But he worked with tools*

*That were not quite right*

*And soon his vision was blurred by the night*

*And as he toiled his purpose was lost*

*And soon he found – he'd fashioned a cross*

*Oh baby sweet – my precious dear*

*I hold you close to hide my fears*

*I wished for a cradle of love for thee*


## MY DARLIN'

*Green are the eyes of my darlin'*

*Green as the restless sea,*

*Warm are the arms that hold me close–*

*And tender his love for me*

*Tall and straight is my darlin'*

*With a smile that quickens my heart*

*The world is mine when I'm in his arms,*

*Ended when we have to part.*

# NEW DAY

*The storm will pass once it's anger's vented*

*And there will be a bright new day–*

*Ah yes it's true,*

*But look now where the storm has lashed*

*Look I say! Don't turn away*

*The tender gentle blooms that die*

*Now withering to dust*

*And trees not strong enough,*

*Are twisted and grotesque*

*Such is the price of anger, fear, and lust*

*Such are the things that dwell in minds like storms*

*And gentle hearts detest*

*But by their fruits you know them*

*And beneath the soft brown earth*

*Protected from the wrath and fury*

*The seeds are planted*

*Take root and grow once more*

*And tho the Mother bloom be utterly destroyed*

*Her children dance as she did long ago upon a silver shore*

# THE NIGHT

*Soft – Soft – the night goes by on quiet muffled feet*

*And tiptoes past my loved ones – lest he disturb their sleep*

*Soft and gentle are my thoughts*

*Wrapped in love for you*

*Sent silently, on wings of prayer*

*To keep you all night thru!*

# NOBLE CREATURE

*A Noble Creature I-*

*I Have Fallen-*

*But- Because - I Reached To Touch The Sky*

*Fallen Now-*

*But Even Now - I'll Try And Try Again*

*I Cannot - Once I've Seen The Start*

*Regard The Plans Of Men-*

*Who Wallow In Their Misery*

*Like Pigs Within Their Mire*

*There Is A Noble Call Within That Bids Me Aim Much*

*Higher*

# NO ROOM FOR ME

*No room for Error? No Room for Me!*

*So keep on searching everywhere–thru Eternity*

*Somewhere, you think, that you will find*

*The perfect one within your mind*

*One who has no faults at all*

*To answer to your beck and call*

*You have judged–and I agree*

*No way, is that person me*

*I was an error!*

*But baby so were you!*

*Two wrongs you say, can't make a right*

*So our love won't do*

*Well right or wrong I love you so*

*Yet deep within my heart I know*

*You do not feel the way I do*

*I cannot make it up to you*

*No room for error!*

*No room for me*

*It fills the air–It fills my soul*

*With bitter agony*

*No room for error–will it ever cease?*

*No room for error–is there no release?*

*No room for error–No Room for Me!*

# NO WAY IN

Ignoring, "all," I deeply feel–

How do I reach you? What is real–

"To you?"

Each time I knock upon the door

Ask to come in – you say

"What for?"

But what else can I do?

Is there some way – I can't define–

Within my heart – within my mind–

To reach you – where you live?

To share with one another

The love we both could give

If – there were not, these "barriers"

Of hurt – and fear – and pain–

Cursed by circumstances time and time again

Would anything be different?

Would I then be – – a part–

Of the love, the hopes, and dreams–

Within your soul – your heart?

I wonder – as I stand outside looking in – at you!–

So don't be angry – if I knock!–

It's all – I know – to do!

Shirley Ann Wood

# NORTHERN LIGHTS

When I was just a child, and first saw, the Northern lights–

I was entranced – as mind and soul filled with pure delight,

Bright radiant colours, dancing there, against a Blackness
deep–

Like visions seen – within a dream when ere I was asleep

The wonder of it, was explained, by my peers, to me–

Tho beautiful – it's nothing more than <u>electricity</u>–

I saw my grandma smile – as she quirked one eyebrow high–

Then I heard her murmur," Angels," – as she gazed upon the
sky

Later, as she heard my prayers – she said Shirley Ann

The lights you saw were angels – people just don't
understand–

Sometimes when all our world is dark filled with fear and
sin,

The littlest Angels – known by man to be the Seraphim

Open up the windows, of Heaven, where they stay–

Creep outside, and in the sky they frolic, laugh and play

The light that streams from heaven shines thru curtains
bright,

Dancing gaily in the sky – lighting up the night–

The crackling sound is laughter – purer than our own,

The colours, reflect – gods love for us

The brightness is his throne.

So when I see the Northern lights–

To this very day –

I think of Grandma's Angels – creeping out to play–

And who's to say that she's not right in her simplicity,

Since all earth and heaven are formed of energy!

## ONE DAY AT A TIME

If I can but delude

Myself for these few hours that make a day

Then I shall be Content

For this day only – is my life!

The Now in which I exist.

Tomorrow an unreality

And as one day follows the other

One Delusion at a Time

One day! This I can bear

My very soul rebels against the mere thought of all the years
to come

Too great the pain of looking so far ahead

Sufficient this second, this minute, this hour, this day

Then when all the days have been completed

Perhaps at last I shall find peace of mind

If not "extinction"

For the Journey of life

*Has left me like the searching Pilgrim*

*Tired, bleeding worn*

*Longing only to know the answer*

*Or failing this, to feel the embrace of*

*Sweet Velvety darkness*

*Where all is nothingness*

*No pain of caring, knowing, trying*

*Just ceasing to be.*

## PARALLEL'S

*I had a dream the other night–*

*A soft voice – spoke to me – and said–*

*" Behold the rose – bush,*

*The meadow, and the tree!*

*Imagine now–*

*The rose – bush with one rose sweet and fair,*

*How perfect would the bloom be–*

*If there were just one petal there?*

*Behold the meadow, lush and green,*

*As its been in ages past*

*Imagine now–*

*How it would be–*

*With just one blade of grass*

*And finally–*

Behold, the tall stately tree!
" Ponder well this knowledge
That I now give to thee"
Imagine now, the tree–
With just a single branch
One loan leaf – is growing there–
Tell me, what's the chance
That all of these, or any,
Could be useful or enhance–
The life that in my wisdom
I've decreed that it should be
A single part of something greater
Rose – bush – meadow - tree.
So my child – my children–
It is the same with all of thee!
Together you are beautiful, so
You must uphold each other
Enjoy the life I've given you
Don't reach to take your brothers!
Be the very best you can
Grow and help to grow!
Accept each blessing as it comes
And you will come to know–
The joy – the satisfaction of being

*Just a part*

*Of one great plan – for all of man*

*To bloom within my heart,*

*Coming to fruition – together–*

*Not alone!*

*For only then – may you approach*

*The pathway to the throne.*

*But if in pride – you stand aside*

*You do not stand for me!*

*For you will be like;*

*The rose –bush, the meadow, and the tree–*

*That has a single petal,*

*One blade, one branch, one leaf,*

*And I shall not look upon you–*

*As in your solitary grief–*

*You live alone,*

*You die alone,*

*Because you could not share*

*In arrogance you turned your back*

*On all who would have cared.*

*So listen now on ponder well*

*The call within your heart*

*The voice of love that bids you,*

*To be – just one small part*

*Of something so magnificent*

*That I have planned for thee!*

*That all will pale, by contrast*

*Rose – bush – meadow – tree!*

## PASSING MOMENT

*She sits so still – hands folded*

*The ravages of time*

*Have dimmed the beauty of body and face*

*Gone, the gentle grace of youth*

*But in the eyes,-a memory of love*

*There for all the world to see*

*And there abiding with it loneliness–*

*And in that moment before the eyes are shyly lowered*

*A silent cry – please! Speak to me*

*Speak young lady that I may form in words once more*

*All that I held dear–*

*And the years will vanish*

*And bring my loved ones once more near*

*So speak to me and you will give the best gift that you can give*

*A moment in the span of time*

*While I, my life, relive!*

Shirley Ann Wood

# PEACE OF MIND

*Spring was near but not yet here*

*And as I gazed around, though the promise you*

*was there in the clean fresh air*

*Snow still lay on the ground*

*The high board fence and the cherry trees*

*looked bleak and so forlorn*

*Not a creature stirred*

*Not a sound could be heard*

*on that bleak and barren morn*

*High side as I shuffled through*

*the snow past raspberry canes,*

*And I wondered as I would with head held low,*

*would spring ever come again?*

*And thereby my feet in tiny splendor*

*grew a cluster of flowers white*

*So pure and fragrant so tiny and sweet*

*they filled me with sheer delight*

*I knelt in snow and gently bowed*

*my head to the spray*

*Of tiny snowdrops growing their*

*on that cold and dreary day*

*And suddenly the day seemed bright*

*And the sun began to shine*

And then I heard the song of a bird
And suddenly joy was mine
For the snowdrops became a promise
Of life renewed, reborn,
So if someday you're feeling lonely and forlorn
Just kneel down and bow your head
And you will surely find
In and said their two-year silent prayer
For joy and peace of mind

## PERCEPTION

I am what you think I am. It's true
What you think I and that's what I am – to you
It's all in your mind as people say.
The way you think of me that's how I am today
Have I been kind have I been mean?
Made you laugh, or cry and scream
No matter what I think I am no matter what I do,
I cannot alter how you think, or what I am to you
And so each day, in every way I'm just a memory
Within your mind I end up being what you think of me
And yet I hope by every single thing I say or do
The memory you have of me and what I am to you
And so I try so very tired to be what I should be

*So you will think I am the person*
*I want so much to be*

# THE PLACE

*She Stands By The River, And Suddenly–Time*
*Sweeps Her Backward, In, Her Memories,*
*Thru Tears In Her Eyes, She Sees Summer Blue Skies*
*And Blossoms, On Knarled Apple Trees,*
*She Sees Dad In His Hammock, The Car In The Drive,*
*Opens The Door And Walks Softly Inside,*
*Of A Home–That Once Used To Be*
*It's All Just The Same As The Joy And The Pain*
*Mingle In Sweet Memory!*
*Caught Up In Her Dream, Of So Long Ago*
*She Follows The Sound Of The Old Radio*
*Playing One Of Her Favorite Tunes.*
*Mom's, Sitting There, Curled Up In Chair*
*As Her Brother Walks Into The Room!*
*She Stays For Awhile–Then Tenderly Smiles,*
*Leaves–To Gather One Last Memory*
*By The River He Stands–As He Takes Her Hand*
*He Whispers–Please–Always Love Me!*
*She Touches His Cheek, His Sweet Mouth She Seeks,*
*Two Bodies–One Spirit–So True!*

*Was It That Long Ago? She Whispered*

*You Know! My Darling! I'll Always Love You!*

*Then, She, Held Him Tight–For The Oncoming Night*

*Sent A Chill, To Her Heart, And Her Bones,*

*Tho She Wished It To Stay, Her Dream Slipped Away,*

*And She Stands By The River–Alone!*

*So Much Of Life Gone–What Use To Go On?*

*Perhaps She Should Linger–Or Stay?*

*But It's Now Fantasy–What Once Used To Be*

*So She Turns–And Walks Slowly Away*

*She's No Longer Young–And Not Very Smart*

*Or She'd Follow Her Head Instead Of Her Heart*

*But Then That Would Mean She Never Would Feel*

*The One Thing In Life That's Worthwhile, That Is Real*

*The Sweetness Of Love*

*That Leads Us To Bleed–If We Must*

*For We Trust In Such Love*

## PLAY ON WORDS

*Rain, Wind, Snow, Sleet,*

*Anger, Fear, Pain, Defeat*

*Summer, Fall, Winter, Spring,*

*Laughter, Colour, fun, being*

*Feel, Hear, Touch, See,*

*Love, Music, Smooth, Free*

*Father, Mother, Child, GOD,*

*Strength, Softness, Sweet, Nod*

*Bend, Kneel, Bow, Pray,*

*Patience, Wait, Hope, Day*

*Day of Destruction?*

*Or Day of Birth?*

*Life of Sorrow?*

*Or Life of Mirth?*

*Play on Words, Play on Minds!*

## POMPOUS.

*Fat Pious Pig telling all the world what they should do.*

*Bulbous creature sweating, spitting out your views between
your yellowed teeth.*

*Ostentatious, overbearing, narrow-minded views that begin
and cease with you.*

*How have you fed the mortal body indulging its every
desire.*

*Pampered it, sought all it craved, burning food, luxuries, sex
in an unending lustful fire*

*But what of thy immortal soul that lives when flesh is dead
and gone*

*Why have you ignored its needs, when it is half of you*

*A delicate gentle lovely part like some ethereal Song*

*The God Part – Nay – you will not even say it, acknowledge it is there*

*For God to you is all you own. The rest is as the air.*

*Ignored tho vital, fool, fat fool, you will not even bend a knee.*

*Too Proud –of what? Do you not know although the world may cater to thy vanities*

*Behind your back they laugh at thee?*

*Poetry, music, philosophy, a blue sky up above,*

*Prayer, patience, sympathy, art, devotion, love.*

*These are a few of the things that feed the soul*

*Meditating on the gentle aspects of this life*

*Bring you closer to the goal*

*That God intended we should seek.*

*So turn that fat and Florid Cheek*

*Just Once!*

*And you may learn a lesson in Humility*

*Do not and you will add more scars to an already over-burdened, suffering humanity*

*So for Man's sake – For God's Sake*

*Give some thought to what you do*

*Unimportant – important man our world*

*Our fate, rests on decisions made up of*

*Good or Evil – Proud or Humble millions*

*Great or Simple, Single men such as you*

# POOR LITTLE ONE

*Poor Little One–*

*Standing so forlorn*

*Not blessed with beauty or high intelligence,*

*Left dirty, neglected, clothes rumpled and torn*

*Heart aching because you just don't understand*

*The standards by which you are judged*

*And found lacking by your elders*

*Superior MAN*

*Eyes beseeching, hope dying each day that you live*

*That someone, just anyone, will comfort and give*

*The love and care you so desperately need*

*But tho your heart reaches out and your soul fairly pleads*

*You are pushed in the background with no one to care*

*That you feel, that you're lonely, or even just there!*

*Poor Little One,*

*Dear little innocent heart,*

*Just because you are different you're set far apart*

*Sweet angel beset by confusion and fear*

*You cry silently, scream loudly–and no one to hear!*

# PREJUDICE

*I'll kill you cause you're Black*

*I'll kill you cause you're White*

*I'll kill you cause you're Yellow*
*In the dead of the night.*
*I'll hate you cause you're Christian*
*I'll hate you cause you're Jew*
*Whatever your religion*
*You'll know that I hate you.*
*And so the world proclaims it right*
*To hate and kill their Brother*
*Tho God has said through ages past*
*"You must love one another"!*

## PRIDE GOETH BEFORE A FALL

*Humpty Dumpty sat on a wall*
*But what made Humpty Dumpty fall—*
*It was me, I'm the cause of it all—*
*I'm the gal who made him fall,*
*What right had he to sit up there?*
*Being such a snot and square?*
*So I decided then and there*
*I'd put an end to it all*
*So I dressed up in my best bib and tucker*
*And I took a stroll right after supper*
*It was such a romantic night*
*With a lovely moon so full and bright*

And when I strolled past that big brick wall

I knew that Humpty was going to fall

And very soon he tumbled down

With a terrible thud, he struck the ground

His ego was shattered beyond repair,

For he looked so silly just lying there

And as the crowd gathered round to see

A shattered Humpty spoke sadly to me

Only love can shatter the proud

And only a fool looks down on the crowd

If I'd only taken my rightful place

I wouldn't be here with this egg on my face.

## PRISMS

Some people are like prisms

On whom the light of life doth play

Reflecting glory everywhere

Each and every day – They live!

They capture all the wonder

That was meant for us to know

The many facets of their lives

Reflect, and lovingly bestow

The beauty that they radiate

Because they never keep, but give

*Each lovely beam of life*

*And help us all to live*

## QUANDARY

*Would that I had some power-*

*To turn this fantasy-*

*This useless life of pain and strife*

*Into reality-*

*Reality in which to live*

*Where I could take - recede or give*

*And not me judged by me-*

*God-Why did - you bless and curse me-*

*With a soul that's not divine*

*But wants to be in spite of me*

*Like yours - and not like mine?*

*Why is it? When I follow you*

*I fail - I hurt – Then I fall thru*

*All reason - to the pits*

*Of darkness and despair*

*In spite of love - believes in you*

*There is nobody there!*

*I walk alone-so alone*

*I'm lonely in this place-*

*I long for love for truth*

*For light - and your heavenly grace*

*But you have left me all alone*

*You have left me on my own*

*I cannot find my way-*

*I call you there's no answer*

*So I'm alone –again- today!*

## THE QUEST

*"She walks in beauty like the night"*

*Once a poet said*

*The beauty of these words live on*

*Tho the Poet's dead*

*Once a Painter saw a face*

*That stirred a deep desire*

*Deep within the Artist's soul*

*To give paint living fire*

*So on a virgin canvas*

*Beauty gained release*

*The whole world vied, to own it*

*The Artist's Masterpiece*

*Once a young Composer*

*Heard within his soul*

*Wondrous music yet unheard*

*For he alone did know*

*The form it took*

*As note by note within his Artist's mind*

*It fit together, became whole*

*Sonata, for mankind*

*And there are others – dreamers all*

*Answering a special Call*

*To endow the human race*

*With Beauty, Music, Poise and Grace*

*And how it feels to care!*

*So on and on the circle goes*

*And on and on the circle grows*

*Adding others of mankind*

*With Artists' souls and Artists' minds*

*Attempting in this Breath called Life*

*To stem the tide of fear and strife*

*Heeding one great call*

*To Portray in their own way*

*What lives within us all*

*The spark – that from creation*

*Drives man to seek, to find*

*The path that leads to Eden*

*That somewhere in his mind*

*Remains like some lost memory*

*The Amnesia of our race*

Yet here and there we find a clue

Leading to this place

God grant someday we find it

Tho the path is hard and long

Spirits need uplifting thru Dancing, Jest and Song

Or _any_ form of Beauty that _anyone_ can give

Just one small kindness

Actors – Living on their stages

Other lives from Living pages

Skaters, dancers, acrobats

Graceful as young jungle cats

That sylphlike stalks

Or leaps and bounds

Landing lightly, without sound

Architects that search to find

Within the castles of their mind

The perfect Structure – their design!

Clowns that seek to prove their Worth

With their wondrous gift of Mirth

Singers, changing simple notes-

Pouring forth from honeyed throats

Words that take us deep inside

Like a magic carpet ride

To anytime or anyplace

A special feeling, special face

They sing the words that someone wrote

Because <u>they</u> wished to share

The dreams, the hopes, the love

The pain, the faith, or deep despair

They felt when they went deep inside

In this life, you've been meant to live

Will make the journey easier

For <u>someone</u> that you've known

And they'll remember, they'll remember

When they, at last find home

And their Father he will listen

To their tale of life

He'll know the ones who loved His Son

And those who caused Him Strife

He'll look at all the souvenirs

Brought back from Planet Earth

Some bought with Blood or Stained with tears

Some dyed with Love and Mirth

Some beautiful beyond compare

Some simple things found anywhere

Some He'll treasure – some discard

It will depend on you

He gave you life and with that life

*What did you choose to do?*

*In you works did you portray*

*The Artist that was you*

*Or are the things you should have done*

*Left standing Stark and Bare*

*Covered with the Dust of Time*

*As if you were not there?*

*How much – how little do you care?*

*As I laugh, I cry*

*He laughs , He cries.*

## RAVE ON

*Well the little things you say and do*

*Make me want to be with you*

*Rave on it's a crazy feeling*

*And I know it's got me reeling*

*When you say I love you rave on*

*The way you dance and hold me tight*

*The way you kiss and say goodnight*

*Rave on it's a crazy feeling*

*And I know it's got me reeling*

*When you say I love you rave on*

*I'm so glad you're revealin'*

*Your love for me*

*Rave on, rave on and tell me*

*Tell me not to be lonely*

*Tell me you love me only*

*Rave on with me*

## REALITY

*We live in a reality*

*Where death is the finality*

*The end of all our striving to achieve*

*For in the short time we are here*

*The angels watch, while in our ear*

*The hissing of the Serpent still is near*

*But tho we've lost all power*

*There is a promised hour*

*We know not when*

*All this, shall cease to be*

*The children of the light*

*Shall be taken from the night*

*To a world of God's reality*

*Where there is no pain*

*No monetary gain*

*In torturing the helpless ones of earth*

*If not for gain – then fun*

*All of this is done*

*By those who create these living hells*

*But what they wish upon one another*

*A helpless animal or brother*

*Shall be their self earned portion from the well*

*For as ye give shall ye receive*

*This is ordained – thru God! A certainty!*

*No one can buy the source,*

*Entice, deceive or force*

*God turns His back on all of those who try*

*But grace from His great throne*

*Shall flow down upon His own*

*And heal the helpless in the twinkling of an eye*

*Some think this will not be*

*That it is a fallacy*

*And if not, they will never see the day*

*So they do what ere they choose*

*Thinking they can't lose*

*They'll take it all and never have to pay*

*They don't seem to know*

*By their free will they'll go*

*To the place they caused another one to be*

*For the Spirit doesn't cease*

*Love is its release*

*Without love – God!*

*I hope I never see*

# REGRETS

*I didn't believe you*

*When you said you loved me*

*How could I believe that was true?*

*For once my heart was broken*

*When such words were spoken*

*By someone I thought I knew.*

*I loved him so much*

*Thrilled to his touch*

*Never dreaming that things could go wrong,*

*But he walked away*

*And nothing I could say*

*Would bring back the love and the song.*

*So I learned to hide*

*To live deep inside*

*Away from the friends I once knew*

*Where no one could touch me*

*So no one could hurt me*

*By saying these words–*

*I LOVE YOU!*

*But I need to know*

*In spite of my pain*

*That someday and somehow*

*I'll be loved again.*

*So make me believe you*

*When you say "I love you"*

*Make me thrill to your love and your touch*

*Make me laugh, make me cry*

*Feel I just want to die*

*If you didn't love me so much!*

## REMEMBER ME

*Oh my love I knew you for one brief moment in the span of time*

*Felt your tenderness surround me, held close within your arms*

*And lost myself in eyes that saw the passions that were mine*

*No words were needed just a touch a glance and we walked on paths known only to angels-for so God and desired men to be*

*Man and Woman with one mind in understanding*

*Needing- giving- longing to prolong such ecstasy*

*Ah the joy of loving deeply with the soul and being loved so in return*

*A gift beyond all riches here on earth*

*Of such is heaven made and lacking such a love all mankind yearns-for*

*Such as this we were designed-"I came" he said-*

*That you may have life more abundantly Love he meant-*

*Once I knew it-long years ago when loves surrounded me*

*But like a child I tired-turned my back and walked away*

*following the path that wound, playing in the sunshine of*
*my youth*

*and soon was lost and crying all alone-*

*take away the night, send back the day!*

*But to a child the night is ages long cold and frightening and*
*finally exhausted*

*it falls asleep hoping soon warm arms will hold it close*
*once more*

*Perhaps! But now the seeds are sown - doubt and*
*fear- uncertainty-contrite*

*I whisper-I'm sorry*

*If you no longer love me at least remember me*


## REMEMBRANCE DAY

*For power and Glory the Nations Vied,*

*In hunger and pain the children cried,*

*I was a child of the Earth and I died.*

*Remember – Remember, don't ever forget,*

*The price of Freedom was high*

*Great was the sacrifice – great is the debt*

*The future is yours to decide*

*We pray for you always*

*As you pray for us*

*On this – Remembrance day*

*May all men be brothers.*

*And the earth blessed with peace.*

*To survive you <u>must</u> find a way*

*For when you have found it*

*It will be as God planned*

*On that day the great Lion will*

*Lie down with the Lamb.*

## RIGHT FOR YOU

*We never do survive! – completely–*

*Bits and pieces tend to disappear,*

*In our struggle just to stay alive*

*There seems so little time to stop and peer – within!*

*No wonder then, not sure of who we are,*

*We listen to advice from those we know*

*Accept so many of the things they say*

*And following, we never seem to grow*

*We are so varied, from a common seed–*

*Born <u>not</u> to follow, but in compassion <u>lead</u>–*

*<u>The</u> life – <u>Our</u> life – God-given at our birth,*

*Free soul, free will, to find <u>our way</u>, <u>our</u> worth!*

*The others? Tho <u>they</u> may show concern–*

*Teach us what they know, and from us sometimes learn,*

*They have no right to tell us how to live–*

*Demanding things we have no wish to give,*

*So listen to your heart, the voice that dwells within,*

*And you'll discern what's right for <u>you</u>*

*And what – to <u>you</u> is sin!*

*For losing <u>all</u> of what you are – what <u>you</u> were meant to do!*

*Is sin indeed – the greatest one, against one person – <u>you</u>!*

*So <u>share</u> your life – when ere you wish with others of your kind*

*Gi<u>ve</u> your life if so you wish – but do not offer mine*

*For if <u>I</u> wish – <u>I'll</u> offer – what <u>I</u> can give to you,*

*And if you feel it's not enough*

*My offer just won't do–*

*Then say goodbye, remain a friend, and please remember me,*

*As one who loves you, tho at times we often disagree-*

*About the <u>one</u> I really <u>am</u> or <u>you</u> want me to be*

*No more bits and pieces can I afford to lose,*

*So now I search for all I lost – as <u>my</u> own way I choose*

*Not in anger do I go – But go I <u>must</u> you see*

*My own way, In my own time, to choose what's right for me!*

*But should you like the way I am –*

*And in you I see, a soul mate, who can offer*

*A better life for me,*

*Then we can walk together in perfect Harmony,*

*For will I be, just as I wish, to mine own self so true,*

*And in turn be happy that it's the same with you*

*Growing strong together –*

*In acceptance - and in Love –*

*With faith in one another and guidance from above*

*So choose without a single qualm*

*What you wish to do – I'll understand*

*That you have chosen – what is <u>right</u> for <u>you</u>!*

## SACRIFICE

*Thinking it was noble*

*I spent my very life*

*Struggling to be the best,*

*Daughter – Mother – Wife!*

*But of course I couldn't be–*

*All that they would wish of me–*

*However I succeeded to let them have their way,*

*So week by week, month by month,*

*Every single day!*

*I struggled with the selfish wish*

*That lived inside of me*

To show this world and tell this world

There is no more to me–

Than the Daughter – Wife and Mother–

You know me to be

But is there? Well there _was_–

But that was long ago

This person that you see–

The one you claim to know!

She sometimes makes you angry

Often makes you sad

Sometimes makes you happy

Often makes you mad

And then there are times

When you can't cope with me

But that's because I'm really _not_

The person that _you_ see!

I am a coward first of all

That's given in to others call

Never daring once to be

The one who lives inside of me

What is she like?

This creature torn

Moody, angry, and forlorn–

Beginning life a special child

Shirley Ann Wood

*With great potential*

*Running wild,*

*In control of all she does*

*With mind so bright and clear–*

*Then suddenly the touch of death*

*Fills her heart with fear*

*But changeling now – she cows and bows*

*For all the world to see*

*Not much left of all she was,*

*This person who is me*

*Of all she was – it's only pride*

*That stays with her*

*That still survives–*

*And tho the rest is lost and gone*

*With pride alone she carries on.*

*But pride must fall and so must she–*

*And so there's nothing left of me*

*Except the one you know – and see*

*The one who lives <u>outside</u> of me*

*Who, like a puppet on a string*

*Lives each day for <u>you</u>*

*So tell me what to say,*

*Tell me what to do*

*Tell me how to live my life*

I need you now – you see

For I am you- and you-

I am no longer me!

I tried with all my will

To make myself survive

But you were stronger, so you live

And me ?

Who me ? I died!

## THE SACRIFICE

The night has gone

Yet day is not yet here

The world is hushed

Its dawn

Soft mist and light diffuses the darkness

Beginning another day

A time of solitude

To think – remember – pray

Yet knowing

Accepting this beginning might

Bring harsh reality

As He did know

So long ago

In the garden of Gethsemane

*That He begged the bitter cup*

*He would not have to taste*

*Yet drank the full of it*

*The anger of the multitude*

*Laid His body waste*

*Then spit upon Him in their anger*

*Thinking they had won*

*When at last they heard Him say*

*"Father it is done!"*

*Save yourself – they jeered Him*

*He can't – He's just a man*

*They'd done their worst*

*But His spirit lived*

*Christianity began*

*So if you are called a dreamer, a fool*

*Condemned as useless and weak*

*So even was the Son of God*

*As He turned the other cheek*

*A waiting time*

*Then He rose again*

*In the hush of another dawn*

*A promise*

*He would someday return*

*The quietly He was gone!*

*He knows how you feel*

*He felt it too*

*Hurt, despair and pain*

*But He conquered all*

*And so can you*

*In His Holy Name!*

## THE SAME FOR YOU

*How Is It? You Can Simply" Be!"*

*Yet Touch The Very Soul Of Me!*

*Just Your Smile Can Make Me Sigh*

*By One Word Live - Another Die!*

*I Guess I'll Never Understand*

*That When You Simply Reach, To Touch My Hand*

*The World's A Better Place*

*You've Shown Me How To Deal With Things*

*I, Once Just Could Not Face!*

*You've Made Me Know - You've Made Me Grow*

*In Wisdom, Courage, Love-*

*You've Led Me From "My Dark Place*

*And Placed My Heart Above-*

*The Fear, The Pain, The Deep Despair-*

*That Was My Life - (When You Weren't There)*

*You're More Than Husband, Lover-*

*You Are My Staunchest Friend-*

*So Once More, As I've Said Before-*

*Time And Time Again !*

*In All Emotions - Honour Me-*

*With Truth ! No Matter - What It Be!*

*In All The Ways - Be True-*

*And I Shall Always - In All Things - Do The Same For You.*

## SEARCHING

*I listened for a symphony*

*And heard discordant sounds,*

*I reached my hands up to the Stars,*

*But tore them in the ground*

*I longed to talk to someone*

*But such babble everywhere –*

*Blocked out the single voices*

*So no secrets could I share*

*So I knelt and spoke to God*

*Who can stay the mighty storms*

*And tho lonely sad and tired*

*My heart once more was warm*

*So shall I seek and hope to find*

*Some truths – what 'ere they be*

*And maybe – sometime – somewhere*

*Someone who thinks like me.*

*Someone who'll stop to share a thought*

*And wait for my reply*

*Who looks in the heart of a flower*

*And wonders at the sky!*

## SEASONS OF MANKIND

*And so we do what we must do*

*Until another day is thru*

*Tho its demands be great or small*

*We must respond to fill them all*

*For we who wake, each day must give*

*Of what we can, each day we live*

*For like each day, our destiny*

*Is just to rise, to live, to be!*

*And when our day has run its course*

*And gentle night descends*

*What have we left behind us?*

*When we cannot make amends!*

*Or do we need to? Maybe not!*

*You see it all depends*

*The day is yours – and yours alone*

*To choose what it shall be*

*My day could be far different*

*It will be up to me*

*I cannot blame you if it's bad*

*And so in turn you see*

*You must take upon yourself, responsibility*

*For the life that's but a day – in the span of time*

*Each one special in its way – unique in its design*

*Like a maiden, sweet and shy*

*Dawn blushes softly thru the sky*

*Just before the day begins*

*With a bright and golden grin*

*There is a quiet interim*

*When there is no sound at all*

*Among the silent trees*

*Until a meadowlark's sweet call*

*Entices forth a breeze*

*That scatters diamond dew drops*

*From emerald coloured leaves*

*Bright flowers shake their tousled heads*

*And from their warm and tumbled beds*

*Children rise to greet the day*

*Too drowsy yet to run and play*

*They rouse their peers – or suck their thumb*

*No hurry – day has just begun!*

*But morning mists – caught in the dell*

Are vanishing, will soon dispel

As like the night – they must give way

To the new, persistent day

Born of dawn it fills the land

Waking all with its demands

As day by day we forge the years

Thru seasons of mankind


## THE SEED

I am a seed - A wildflower seed

Of not much worth

I lie alone beneath the warm dark earth

I know within that I could grow

Reach into another world

And I cry deep inside because it is not so.

The earth is packed too hard above me

No rain or sun just darkness fills my world

I strain – I yearn – but nothing helps me

Oh God I cannot do it all alone

No creature – <u>nothing</u> grows unless someone knows

The hard packed earth must first be broken

Soft rain must fall gently caressing, coaxing

With the sun its partner in life

Then the will to be just something

*Will make the ultimate bloom*

*Worth all the strife*

*For sweet the scent as it nods its head*

*In the soft warm summer's breeze*

*Small accomplishment – maybe –*

*But the joy the freedom just to be*

*God – listen – heed*

*I strive, I long – To Be!*

*TO BE!*

## SEEING YOU

*They See You Standing Small*

*I See You Standing Tall*

*They Cannot Understand That Once When I So Needed It*

*You Smiled And Took My Hand*

*They Look To See The Things Of Earth*

*They Cannot See The Things Of Worth*

*The Noble Spirit, Noble Pride*

*That Causes Noble Ones To Hide All Mistakes And Pain*

*Inside!*

*Counting All Mistakes A Sin*

*Head Held Aloft They Joke And Grin*

*Allowing None To Peer Within*

To See The Pain The Sorrow There The Loneliness - The Deep
Despair

They Must Recede, To Rest And Find

Within Their Heart, And Soul And Mind

The Truth About Their Aims, Their Worth

The Legacy Of Noble Birth

Like A Racehorse In It's Prime

They Will Run - And Win - This Time

We Know You Will, We Understand

For When You Reached To Touch Our Hand

You Also Reached Into Our Heart

And Made Us All A Tiny Part Of Something Greater given
All

(With The Courage To Stand Tall)

That Noble Efforts Never Fail And Noble Spirits Never
Quell

Perhaps There's Some Who Deem Them Small

Because They Never Will Stand Tall

In Fact They'll Never Try At All

But Try You Will For Try You Must

For To You In Holy Trust

Was Given Courage To Go On And Pride In Being Jon

Big Jon!

Shirley Ann Wood

## SET FREE

*You told me today–you must go away*

*And darling I guess that you do*

*You must walk alone, for a while on your own*

*To yourself you must start to be true*

*I know this is so–but how to let go*

*When my heart is filled with such pain,*

*Each moment I feel is just so unreal*

*Things never will be quite the same*

*There's nobody else I can turn to*

*That could ever mean so much to me*

*So how to let go when I love you so*

*Yet must for your sake set you free*


## SHE STOOD

*"She Stood" - - In Silent Majesty !*

*Her very "presence" - deemed–*

*The slipping of reality*

*Into a world of dreams-*

*"In Which!" All things that "could have been"*

*All things - that still "could be"*

*Were beautiful , and warm and real-*

*"So Like" - the Fantasy-*

*He'd hold within his heart so long*

That only He could see!

Yet now, within this moment, as cruel years slipped away-

In faith the power surged within - Love beckoned him to stay-

And truth as pure as nectar gave him back the key-

To all the things - That "could have been"

To all - - that - - still - "could be!"

For that single moment, His Soul "Believed", "rejoiced!"

Then came, unbidden - from his fears - a stark and dreadful voice-

This is not real - it's just a dream - leave - and follow me

Then as he turned once more he faced - His "True" – Reality

## SILENT ANGUISH

Descended from seafarers -Those mighty men of old

Salt for blood, Strength of steel

Adventurous and Bold! We are Newfoundlanders

And we shall always be -As we've been in ages past

Children of the sea!

For centuries we've lived along - our great Atlantic shore,

For centuries we've pulled our net's, and laid against our oars,

But now we are forbidden to fish our waters fair

We've over-fished they tell us, and the fish are just not there-

*Our vessels have been dry-docked, and we're told to understand*

*That we must all find other lives - no choice - but stern command*

*So long we spoke of draggers that ripped our ocean floor*

*And tankers with their oil spills contaminating shores*

*We pleaded - please do something - save our beloved sea*

*Yet those of greed - Not of need - destroyed our legacy*

*Why were they not dry-docked? Told to understand-*

*They could not -In one lifetime destroy the sea and land*

*That had for centuries provided livelihood for all*

*Not just the few who used their gold - like a siren's call*

*To blind the ones of power who could have intervened*

*But they did not - and so today our dories drift a sea*

*Where not a single fish can be caught by you or me*

*Surrounded now by ghost ships - I seem to hear a song*

*Something of a last farewell*

*That Fades – And Then–*

*Is Gone!*

## SONG OF LOVE

*Remember me from long ago?*

*The simple girl you used to know?*

*The one who prayed to God above*

To find a boy that she could love!

The girl who dreamed and cried and laughed,

Exploring every wondrous path?

Innocence personified! Do you remember when she died?

It was an agonizing death, terminal, and long,

First went the dreams, and then the hope,

And finally the song!

The song of life she'd loved so much

With music from the spheres,

Eternal words of majesty

To guide her thru the years!

There came the sounds of discord

That clamoured to be heard

Distortions of her music

Destruction of her words

They said she had no place–this girl of long ago,

That she must suffer–face the facts

So that she might grow

Grow in understanding of true reality

Throw off the clock of innocence

That dwelt in Fantasy

And tho she fought with all her heart

She could not win the fight

So in the desert–all alone–thru the endless night

*Once again she prays, to God who dwells above–Lord*

*"Help me find, peace of mind," within your song of Love*

*Amen!*

## SOUL MATES

*I will not stay with you*

*If there's no love for me*

*I cannot dwell within the cold,*

*But to the warmth will flee*

*Risking all–to be a part*

*Of A Tender, Loving Heart*

*I'll search forever, if I must*

*Until I find the peace of mind*

*In someone I can trust!*

*For I cannot be owned or bound*

*Nor shall I ever be*

*By one who'd chain me to the ground,*

*And kill the soul of me*

*I'll give you anything you ask*

*Whatever you desire*

*But only if your shelter's warmed*

*By love's sweet gentle fire*

*Even then, I'll leave sometimes*

*Don't wonder if I do*

*For if you really love me*

*I shall return to you!*

*I'll only leave–when I am restless*

*To spread my wings in flight*

*Or ponder stars by night*

*To stay a little while with God*

*The one who counsels me*

*"You are my daughter, born of love*

*A creature wild and free–and*

*Tho sometimes–you're hurt I know*

*Just keep your faith and you will grow*

*For I'll be by your side*

*Only love can claim you*

*So live where love abides*

*Tis then, I shall return love,*

*Because I long to be*

*Within the heart of one who cares*

*And shares, his love with me*

*A tender place–to call my own,*

*A gentle place–that I call "Home"*

*With you–My Destiny!*

Shirley Ann Wood

# SPECIAL

*It seems so long ago I met you*

*One lovely summer's day*

*You touched my soul and claimed my dreams*

*With what you had to say*

*To some it wouldn't mean a lot,*

*For me it swayed my heart*

*You said I was the special one,*

*That we would never part!*

*Now time has passed, and thru the years*

*Of work and laughter, fun and tears*

*All was good–in it's own way*

*Except today–*

*I am not special!*

*Different yes! Yet still the same,*

*Except for thoughts and face and name*

*I could be them! They could be me!*

*Their moment–My Eternity*

*When they were–someone special!*

*You do not seem to know,*

*You cannot seem to see,*

*The moment that they took my place*

*They defeated me!*

*You say my love was stronger*

And therefore I have won

In winning, I have less by far

Then when we first begun

The bitter cost of what I've lost

They call Reality

And from now on that dreadful truth

Will always dwell with me

And tho I love you–always will

I never more will be–

Special!

## I'M SPECIAL

I'm special if you love me

And tell me this is so

If not, I'm nothing special

With nowhere then to go

For there could be no other

To fill the special place

That is reserved within my heart

For you – <u>your</u> special place

## STORYBOOK

I'm growing oh so weary, for I am growing old,

I've known so many folks along the way.

*But before the Story's ended, and the book is closed*

*There are some things that I would like to say-*

*I'd like to thank the ones who've been as tender*

*Each time I've had to walk a trying mile*

*They took my hand and helped me when I stumbled*

*And within my heart they gently tucked a smile*

*And others, who helped me carry burdens, that were too heavy just for me alone*

*The ones who gave me roses to brighten up my day,*

*I'd like to thank each one that I have known*

*There are so many times, so many faces-*

*Countless numbers that have filled my life*

*The ones who've given of their love and laughter*

*And then the others - who give pain and strife*

*Their gifts to me have taught me my lessons*

*Ones I wish sometimes, I'd never known-*

*Uncertainly, and fear, despair and bitter tears,*

*And the panic of surviving - all alone!*

*Whatever gift you give is your decision*

*As you place it in another's heart and soul*

*It is theirs to keep - to make them smile or make them weep*

*To make them cowards, or courageous, Strong and bold*

*So if you think that what you are is just your business*

*And you have the right to do each thing you do*

Remember - what you do and say, every hour of the day Is a
gift of Joy or Sadness made by you

So now the time has come to close the cover

And place my book of life upon the shelf

If it remains to gather dust, or is referred to as a must

I have formed it's worth or lack of it myself-

If I have made the book too grim and heavy

In vain they'll try to move it - for a while-

There is great despair, they'll finally leave it there

Like some great stone bequeathed them - Not a Smile!

But should the book be filled with gentle caring,

It will be opened many times throughout their years,

And within the pages there'll be rainbow pictures,

To delight and even colour tender tears-

And if these many gages filled with loving words and
pictures

Perhaps they'll find compassion and forgive

The many faults and foolish errors,

And the stupid things I didn't do or did.

### SUNLIGHT

We were young

The day was bright

The world was young

As sunlight

*Dappled thru the trees*

*A gentle summer breeze*

*Kissed my lips*

*Caressed me*

*Softly – Bringing forth*

*Anticipation*

*Later Love – You'd*

*Lay with me.*

## SWEET SIXTEEN

*Star studded magic of a winter's night*

*Gliding, sliding over the ice,*

*Suddenly you feel you're falling*

*Mary Lou is gaily calling*

*Laughter's all around you now*

*Kindly laughter from the crowd*

*Up the ice you see him coming*

*Then your heart is sweetly humming*

*As he lends a helping hand*

*You're so in love and gee it's grand*

*Now you're whirling, swirling, floating*

*As his arm around you steals*

*You gaze at him, your eyes are glowing.*

*Can such a magic night be real?*

*Someone's singing, fire's burning*

*In your heart a tender yearning*

*To keep this magic winter night*

*When you're sixteen and all is right!*

## SWEET THING

*Sweet thing I worry about you.*

*Sweet thing I can't live without you.*

*You brighten my day,*

*Make easy my way.*

*Because sweet thing there's something about you.*

*How can I explain the sun when it rains,*

*The joy and the love in a heart filled with pain.*

*Sweet thing I'll love you forever.*

*Sweet thing, abandon you never.*

*In my heart you hold sway,*

*'Til my dying day.*

*Cause sweet thing such love is forever.*

*Cause sweet thing such love is forever.*

## TELL ME WHY

*0*

*In spite of any fault*

*You may have found in me*

*There was no question of my love*

*Or – my loyalty!*

*And tho the path was often hard*

*For you – I persevered!*

*Considering it all – worthwhile*

*Through love – those many years!*

*I gave you – all I had to give*

*Each and every day*

*I lived – the best that I could live*

*Each and every way!*

*But tho it was – all – that I had!*

*'Twas not – enough – for you!*

*The fault – or faults, you found in me*

*You claim – made you – untrue!*

*You said I must not question*

*This longing to be free*

*You said I must not speak a word*

*Just – "let me" – "be me!"*

*Each word you spoke – was like a blow*

*From a heavy stone*

*Brought to my knees in fear and pain*

*I found myself – alone!*

*In my degradation – I uttered one last cry!*

*What fault? Caused you to stone me?*

*In God's name – tell me why!*

# THANK GOD

Lord I thank you for the love I have known—

And humbly thank you for the love <u>You</u> have shown

You gave me a body to work and to feel—

And all the wonders of earth you wished to reveal—

Eyes to see all the wonders around

Ears to hear the numberless sounds

Limbs to carry me over your earth

And others to prove my love and my worth

A womb to carry, protect and produce

Your wondrous creations sent for your use

For all are created to fit in your plan

Found in the beginning, your desire for man—

To acknowledge and thank you for the love you have shown

To be grateful for each touch of love we have known

For only in love is the touch of <u>your</u> hand

The love of a woman

The love of a man

The seed that brings forth

Yet another to love

And we lift our eyes to the realm up above—

And ask for your guidance for all in this land

To follow with trust your wondrous plan

To taste all the sweet things you want us to know

*To weep in compassion – to love and to grow*

*In union with you, so our love may be blessed*

*And when life is over and we're laid to rest*

*May we not be remembered for those words on a stone*

*But instead for the love we have given and shown!*

*When others spoke the many words*

*That are supposed to mean so much*

*In silent understanding–*

*<u>You</u> reached out – to touch*

*When they argued, how very much they helped–*

*And who had helped the most*

*<u>You</u> took my trembling hand in yours*

*And spoke of love and hope!*

*As they painted grim dark pictures*

*Of what the future held for me*

*<u>Your</u> smile dispelled the darkness*

*And set my spirit free*

*When I failed, they turned their backs*

*As if my failure were their own*

*Twas then your arms encircled me*

*So I would not feel alone*

*How can I tell you what it means*

*To be in deep despair*

*To search among the friends you've known*

*And find the one who's <u>there</u>*

*But what need <u>is</u> there to tell you?*

*For in your loving gentle heart*

*You've accepted all I am*

*So I've become a part–*

*Of all that you believe in–*

*And like the star above*

*That guided men of wisdom*

*You <u>know</u> that wisdom's – <u>love</u>*

*But others cannot see – and so they do not know–*

*They bind themselves to things of earth*

*And so they do not grow.*

*For who would choose in place of that*

*The way of burning fire?*

*A path of crucifixion–*

*Of Dreams? Beliefs? Desires?*

*Only such as you – who are guided from above–*

*to help the lost ones – such as me*

*Thank God for you – for love!*

## THANK YOU

*For a very little while*

*You became a part*

*Of who I am, and what I feel*

*So–from the bottom of my heart,*

*I'd like to thank you darling*

*You're sweet, and good, and kind,*

*I'm proud to say–that for awhile*

*You were a "friend of mine".*

*God Bless you darlin'*

*May I say–I know somewhere,*

*Somehow, someday–*

*You'll meet that lady–fine and true,*

*One you'll feel "is right for you"*

*I truly wish I could have been,*

*That special one–not "just a friend"!*

*Thank you for your dear sweet smile*

*That touched my heart so, for awhile*

*I saw the sun again*

*Found the courage to go on*

*Because of you "My Friend"!*

## THERE WAS A TIME

*There Was A Time, I Loved You*

*But That Was Long Ago*

*And At The Time I Didn't Know*

*I Loved You!*

*It's Just That When I Needed You*

*You Were Always There*

*When The World Abandoned Me*

*You Never Ceased To Care, That I*

*Was Hurt Or Close To Tears*

*Lonely, Tired, Sick With Fear*

*I Never Thought How Often Then, I'd Call*

*To Draw You Near!*

*Took You So Much For Granted*

*Never Even Dreamed*

*There'd Come A Time, Beyond My Will*

*When Fate Would Intervene*

*But Come It Did–And Suddenly*

*You Were No Longer There With Me*

*How Could This Be? How Could This Be?*

*I Felt Such Loss! Such Searing Pain!*

*How Could You Be Gone?*

*To Never See Your Face Again*

*How Could I Go On?*

*You Had Given Me So Much*

*A Smile–A Word–A Gentle Touch.*

*Made Me Feel Safe, Protected.*

*"Dear God Up Above"*

*What Does It Take?*

*To Make Us Know When We Encounter Love*

*Must We Lose Everything That's Sweet*

*And Kind, And Good?*

*To Make Us See What We Should Be*

*To Act The Way We Should?*

*Now I See Thru Tear Filled Eyes*

*In Dreadful Clarity*

*All The Love You Had—You Gave*

*Lavished Just On Me*

*How Could I Know? That I Loved You*

*When I Didn't Even Give A Thought*

*To Any Of The Many Things You Did*

*To Make My World A Brighter Place*

*Each Day In Which To Live!*

*I Only Though Of All I Wanted*

*What It Meant To Me*

*And Now That It's Too Late, To Alter Destiny*

*I Long To Say "I Love You!"*

*And See You Smile At Me!*

*There Was A Time!*

*There Was A Time!*

*For You, No More For Me*

*So Take The Time*

*To Love, To Give, To Share—Your Destiny!*

# THINKING OF YOU

*I have loved you for awhile*

*You made me cry, you made me smile*

*You taught me things I didn't know*

*And in the teaching made me grow*

*—I've been thinking of you—*

*I've been thinking how we met*

*Perhaps we shouldn't have—and yet—*

*I guess it somehow had to be*

*That I'd know you, and you'd know me*

*—I've been thinking of you—*

*I've been thinking how our love was like a song*

*That somehow in the end turned out all wrong*

*How could this be when once it seemed so very right?*

*But now the sun has disappeared and in the night—*

*—I've been thinking of you—*

*Ah my love, we could have shared so many years*

*Made all the sweeter by our laughter and our tears*

*For tho you're gone, there's still one thing I know*

*We have loved—and still love each other So!*

*—I've been thinking of you-*

# THIS WOMAN

*She's Been Loved By The Great*

*And Loved By The Small,*

*But Best Of All!*

*She's Been Loved By "God"–This Woman!*

*She's Been A Sister, Daughter, Mother And Wife*

*A Person, A Friend, Yes All Of Her Life*

*She's Been Something To Someone–This Woman*

*She's Not Always Great, Yet Never Just Small,*

*She May Never Go Down In History At All*

*She Just Is*

*And Will Be–This Woman!*

*"She's Unique"*

*A Bright Thread In The Pattern Of Time*

*She's That Sister, Or Daughter Or Mother Of Mine*

*She's That Person, That Friend, Or Wife That You Know*

*She's A Woman!*

*A Woman Sent To Gentle The Land*

*To Nourish The Babe And Comfort A Man*

*But She's More, So Much More–This Woman!*

*She's The Womb Of Nations, And When Adversity's Near*

*She's Pulled A Plow Or Used A Spear,*

*To Maintain Or Protect What She Hold Most Dear–This*

*Woman!*

*What She Holds Most Dear She's Been Saying Thru Time*

*Just As I'm Saying In This Poem Of Mine*

*"All Those Whom We Love"*

*Thus Its Ever Been*

*Ah But It's Hard In A World Ruled By Men,*

*To Speak Of Mere Love, For They Don't Understand–This*
*Woman!*

*Then She Feels So Small, So Helpless,*

*Alone!*

*"Just A Woman" Who Loves Her Land And Her Home*

*Who Cannot Comprehend The Meaning Of War*

*That Destroys Every Vestige Of All She Stands For–This*
*Woman!*

*Power And Politics, Money And Such*

*Somehow They Don't Seem To Mean Very Much*

*–To This Woman*

*She Only Cares Where Her Heart Resides*

*And Her Heart Always Goes Where Love Abides*

*Who Else Can Fathom This Simple Thought?*

*Yet It Is The Same As Jesus Taught*

*–To This Woman*

*But He Came, This God, In The Form Of A Man*

*To Teach–That Since The World Began*

*"Love" Is The Father's Only Plan*

*And When It Seemed That All Was Lost*

*And They Had Nailed Him To The Cross*
*He Placed His Mother In The Care*
*Of One He Loved, Who Was Standing There*
*As He Said–"Behold This Woman!"*

## TIME ALONE

*Give me a smile or just a word to brighten up my day*
*But let me know you really care, and tell me that I may*
*Soon go shopping for a hat – and as an extra treat*
*Stop in some secluded place and order something strange to*
*eat*
*Something I don't cook at home to suit a gourmet's taste*
*To be savored very slowly knowing there's no need for haste*
*Where I'll be treated as a lady to be pampered for a while*
*And as I nod approval I'll receive a gracious smile*
*Just a single afternoon where for a time I'll be*
*Not Mom or a devoted wife, but the girl I used to be*
*Then I'll return refreshed to enfold you in my arms*
*To work, to love and care for you, to guard you from all*
*harm*
*For Mom and a devoted wife I shall forever be*
*And I shall love you all my dears throughout eternity*
*But there are days when I must have a little time alone*
*And having this be reassured I soon will hurry home!*

## TIRED

*Tired—tired of waiting*

*Tired of hoping, looking*

*For a day that never comes*

*Tired of being, believing, trusting*

*Of nose to the grindstone*

*Sticking to my guns*

*Sick of advice and lectures*

*That lead me here and there*

*And roundabout and in and out*

*And finally—nowhere!—*

*Tired of war, violence, hate*

*Tax bills, and so on*

*Tired of buildings crammed together*

*With no place left to grow on*

*Weary of noise that beats in my brain*

*Over and over like a funeral refrain*

*Mostly I'm tired of fear—afraid of what might be*

*And I wish I could wrap it like a gift*

*And give it back to those who gave it to me.*


*To be the parents of this child*

*This tiny little miss*

*And then each angel passing by*

*Bestowed a loving kiss*

*Then Seraphim and Cherubim escorted her to earth*

*And everyone in heaven smiled*

*At the advent of her birth*

*For the love within her mother's eyes*

*Told them that their choice was wise.*

*Now I'd like to send my blessings too–*

*And all my love to both of you!*

## TO BE

*You say you're trying to be nice,*

*You're trying to be kind, you try so hard to understand*

*You're trying all the time*

*But what you just won't understand is something I've been taught and*

*That is if you try to be*

*You may be sure you're not*

*For if you are, you'll never ever have to try to be*

*You hold the world within your grasp*

*And Love's the Golden Key*

*And if you learn to listen, to help, to care – to see*

*Someday you may not have to try and try and try*

*To BE*

## TO DONNA

*The angels conferred in Heaven*

*About a special child*

*Fair of face, filled with grace--*

*With a wee beguiling smile--*

*The Archangel held it on his lap*

*And with his gavel gave a tap--*

*Now we are agreed--this tiny mite*

*So special here above--*

*Must have a home with someone*

*Who will give it lots of love,*

*And I think perhaps a brother*

*To keep it company*

*The angels smiled and Gabriel knew*

*That one and all agreed*

*So they looked down and saw a young man*

*Strong and kind and good*

*With a wife so sweet she'd proved she was made for*
*motherhood*

*They saw the joy within their hearts*

*That another child would come*

*And they decided then and there*

*These were the very ones*

*To be the parents of this child*

*This tiny little miss*

*And then each angel passing by*

*Bestowed a loving kiss*

*Then Seraphim and Cherubim escorted her to earth*

*And everyone in heaven smiled*

*At the advent of her birth*

*For the love within her mother's eyes*

*Told them that their choice was wise.*

*Now I'd like to send my blessings too--*

*And all my love to both of you!*

## TO MOM

*A seed is an expectation*

*A promise unfulfilled*

*That grows into a seedling*

*With tender care and nature's will*

*Becoming tall and slender*

*As it reaches for the sun*

*Soon it buds and it is now*

*An almost perfect one*

*Then suddenly it blooms*

*And fragrance fills the air*

*A delicate and lovely thing*

*That vanquishes despair*

And as it is with gardens

We too respond and grow

The sun that warms and guides us

Is the love we come to know

We reach for those who love us

And love blooms in return

And tho sometimes the sky may darken

And we bow our heads and yearn

Fear not – for God has willed

That the sun will soon return

And just as petals in a book

Bring back sweet memories

Love is pressed within our hearts

For all eternity

So this day I remember

Sweet memories I recall

The love you gave a seedling

To make her straight and tall

How tenderly you cared for her

From the moment of her birth

And from you – she drew

All beauty, her strength and love – her worth

If she loves it's because of the love that she has known

If she's kind it's because of the kindness she's been shown

*But as she travels on thru life*

*She'll never find another*

*Who'll love her more*

*Or whom she'll love as you dear heart - my mother!*

## TORMENT

*I watched helplessly as the grey swallowed the White*

*The Black swallowed the grey*

*And there was eternal night*

*I cried in protest and tore with bleeding hand and aching heart*

*But in vain - I could not tear the shrouds of night apart*

*I reached out in Blindness seeking the solace of a companions hand*

*But it was like grasping smoke that vanished as you held it and voices dim*

*Like Echoes saying - help yourself - I cannot help*

*I do not understand*

*And then - the loneliness, the fear,*

*That holds you rigid in it's Icy Grip*

*So that you cannot move or think*

*You dare not - for the Whip-*

*of Torment is there ! But Where !*

*Where will it strike?*

*And as you wait, you cower in the Black eternal Night.*

# TOUCH ME

*Touch me – I am real – Complete!*
*A woman who's known success – defeat*
*Who's held a child, held a man–*
*Walked alone in shifting sand,*
*Stood on the rim of a canyon wide*
*Had courage – then had to run and hide.*
*Longed to make a dream come true*
*Walked the extra mile for you–*
*Trusted, doubted, laughed and cried,*
*Kept painful secrets locked inside*
*Touch me I am real*
*Not some fantasy–*
*Of what you'd like–*
*For I must be – what I must be*
*And if you like – just what I am*
*Perhaps this woman and this man*
*Can – with love entwine*

# TREASURES

*Tho today you went away*
*The essence of you–lingered,*
*–Stayed–and became a part–*
*Of memories I treasure*

*Hold gently in my heart.*

*And when the days are lonely*

*Or when the nights are long*

*And it seems there are no dreams–*

*No hope, no love, no songs–*

*'Tis then I shall remember*

*And for a little while*

*You shall be–once more*

*With me–*

*The memory of your smile*

*The essence of your presence*

*Like a Summer day*

*May depart–but in my heart*

*"Never Go Away!"*


## THE UNICORN

*The unicorn is wounded*

*And in its agony*

*It runs and hides*

*Somewhere inside*

*Where once it ran so free*

*It cannot move, so now must go*

*Down paths of memory*

*To a world designed for unicorns*

*With lovely waterfalls*

*Rainbows arching 'cross the sky*

*God reigning over all*

*Star-studded nights*

*Filled with delights*

*That those who love can see*

*Fairy rings and all such things*

*That dwell in fantasy*

*'Tis here – that unicorns belong*

*Not in this world of pain*

*He lifts his eyes – up to the skies*

*As softly falling rain*

*Falls upon his mortal wounds*

*As one last breath he takes*

*Dying to this world of pain*

*He knows he'll soon awake*

*Once again back in his world*

*Of love – and mystery*

*From whence he came, so long ago*

*To dwell with you – with me*

*To bring his wondrous magic touch*

*To those his God loves – oh so much*

*Alas, they could not see*

*His greatest gift – his magic*

*Is love – to set us free*

*But all this magic we deny*

*With one accord – we crucify!*

*Till the unicorn is wounded*

*Filled with mortal pain*

*Then we pray and hope – beseeching*

*Send him back to us again!*

## UNICORN'S POINT OF VIEW

*For mortals are there*

*Who can see*

*Beyond their own reality*

*So tho, with them, I do not abide*

*In love – in dreams*

*Locked deep inside*

*They cannot see me – do not care*

*For all their treasures buried there*

*Abandoned hopes – abandoned dreams*

*Replaced with false and useless schemes*

*Still, I remain, for once you see*

*In their youth – their fantasy*

*I was the guardian of their heart*

*And thus became a living part*

*Of all they could have been*

*The unicorn*

*Of love and hope*

*Lost in forgotten dreams*

# THE UNKNOWN

*A weird yellow evening when the sky is bright–*

*With unreal rays of fading light,*

*Light that dispels each shadow, and seems–*

*Like another world of nightmare and dreams.*

*'Tis then in this odd and eerie glow,*

*A sudden cold feeling of fear seems to grow,*

*And I stand and search the lonely sky–*

*I know not for what and I know not why,*

*But deep within my very soul–*

*The apprehension seems to grow,*

*Everything's too quiet and still–*

*Like the end of time. Or the loss of will,*

*And so I know eventually–*

*I too must face eternity.*

# THE POWER OF LOVE

*Ah love that burns so brightly*

*In my soul*

*A glory that changes all the world*

*And seeks somehow to show*

*The one I love the wonder I now feel*

*Oh if only there were someway to reveal*

*My heart – no words would I need to speak*

*Halting, stumbling phrases, that*

*I must repeat*

*To communicate, like every other*

*Mortal who has lived*

*Do you hear an angel sing?*

*Is the sky a bluebird's wing?*

*Is each bird a turtle dove?*

*That's what it's like to be in love*

*But first there is - our life – a while*

*In which to cry – in which to smile*

*A time he gives – in which to learn*

*To fail, succeed, and thus discern*

*The path that we must go*

*For love of him we must accept*

*All that helps us grow*

*Concern yourselves not with the world*

*Nor its demands of thee*

*If it conflicts with truth – with love*

*With all you're meant to be*

*Know there's just a season in which you have to live*

One small chapter

In the book of life – in which to give

Some solace to an aching heart – a touch

A smile – a prayer

A knowing that you love them

And because you do – you care

It may be all that's offered

As they stand alone

So comfort them with their need

Until they too go home


## A MADMANS DREAM

Is it just a madman's dream!

So am I mad? Or am I sane?

And will I ever live again?

All those I know – say give it time!

And yet dear Lord – this life of mine –

Is coming to a close!

You know there is no time to spare –

For what is left – Dear God! Be there!

Let me feel Your presence near –

To dispel this numbing fear –

That I have lived in vain!

Please God – I beg on bended knees –

*Let me feel again –*

*The certainty that You are there –*

*For those who disbelieve! Despair!*

*Have placed such doubts within my heart,*

*That they have torn my soul apart!*

*So only You can mend – restore!*

*What is left of me –*

*For if You do not intervene – I shall cease to be!*

*And if my life You so divide!*

*That You find, You must decide –*

*I am no use at all –*

*In Jesus' name I beg of You –*

*Do not let me fall –*

*To the nether regions wherein Satan dwells –*

*I could not stand the loss of You –*

*Or the pains of Hell!*

*So if I am not worthy – I beg this boon of Thee*

*Simply wipe me from Your mind –*

*Then I shall cease to be*

*Have mercy on this sinner*

*Who knows not what to do –*

*Except to call – Your holy name –*

*And lean – my Lord on You!*

*For You alone are holy – You alone have worth –*

*And with my last – my dying breath –*

*From this – Your planet earth –*

*I will praise Your holy name –*

*And pray – that when You come again*

*To dwell once more with man –*

*If not I! One of my seed –*

*Shall enter in Your plan*

*To do the things I failed to do –*

*In surety – thru love – for You.*

## LOVE FLOURISHES

*On earth or in heaven it shall flourish and grow*

*For love is of God, His essence, his seed*

*Use it wisely but well, for both worlds have a need*

*For the beauty it brings to each hungry soul*

*And the hope that it brings to mankind as a whole*

*If you don't believe in these things I have said*

*And to you – when you die, all you are is now dead*

*That's not true, for all the things that you taught,*

*Shall live on in others – shall not die and rot*

*Like the shell that you wore while on planet earth*

*But go on thru the decades, be they vile or of worth.*

# YESTERDAY

*Was it just yesterday, I was alive?*

*Yesterday – when I strived, so hard, to please you?*

*And trying to make the day more pleasant*

*Held back tears to gently tease you*

*But you had no time for foolish play*

*More and more work to be done each day*

*Soon tho, we, would be able to play*

*When this or that was done*

*When we could relax and take the time*

*To enjoy the warmth of the sun*

*Then we would not be too weary*

*To look at the stars at night*

# WHAT POWERS?

*What powers stood in shrouds*

*And assisted at my birth?*

*Then mocked my clumsy efforts*

*And impeded me with stumbling blocks*

*As I attempted life on Earth?*

*Who, as I managed to escape*

*Gave them sway to make me stay*

*Then stripped me of my birthright*

*To make life harder still*

*Leaving only vague remembrances*

*Of all I was*

*And my indomitable will*

*A will without direction*

*Except to do what's right*

*Brings a sadness and confusion*

*And night moves thru the night*

*Music, poetry and colors*

*Paint pictures in my mind*

*And so I think and ever search*

*But never seem to find*

*The life that's like a lovely dream*

*A dream I want to share*

*But with whom? When no one will believe*

*That it is even there?*

*And so I must abide by rules*

*That are not even mine*

*And walk, with faltering unsure steps*

*Along with all mankind*

*Why? When I do not even wish it*

*Do I dwell upon this earth*

*What and why this foolish joke?*

*Enacted at my birth?*

# YOU NEEDED ME

*You needed me, I saw this, and I knew,*

*So in love – I tried to help as I walked with you*

*Tho I soon was weary, as your burdens bent me low*

*Still in love – I walked with you for I loved you so,*

*But now you do not need me and the road is long*

*So let me stay – go now love – for once more you are strong*

*Tho you <u>wish</u> I'd stay with you – I do not wish to go*

*Leave me now – in peace I pray – <u>if you</u> love me so!*


# UNTO THY SELF

*I get so angry – when I see–*

*Compassion – "Individually!"*

*Yet ever since the world began–*

*"Man's inhumanity to man!"*

*I've listened to the children cry–*

*Beheld the pain – as nations die*

*As in the effort – "To become!"–*

*<u>Forget</u> – "we are!" – and – "<u>We</u> – Are One"*

*Politics – religion – we always defy*

*– Until the <u>name</u> – becomes – The Game*

*And <u>fails</u> – "To Simplify!"*

*Where there is abundance–*

*<u>So little</u> do we share–*

For those who have a desperate need–

So little do we care!

Ah yes – I've heard all reasons–

That we must sell – give–

Politically it is not sound–

Somehow, Someway –" They'll live!"

Religion must not intervene–

As wolves devour sheep

Appointed shepherds in His name

Wring their hands and weep

## UNTOLD LOVE

I Love You Oh So Much

I Haven't Told You Near Enough

Reached Out To Simply Touch

And Why? I Do Not Know! It Would Have Been So Simple

Instead I Let You Go

Feeling Sad And Lonely, Bewildered And Unsure,

I Should Have Called You Back, But I Was Insecure,

Thinking It Was Over, Wondering Who Was Right Or Wrong

Until Today When Thoughts Of You Came With A Lovely
Song

That Spoke Of Precious Moments, Brief Moments That We
Live

*And How A Single Moment Is All That We Can Give*

*That We Should Share That Moment, For It Will Never Come Again*

*And Love Each Other In It, Instead Of Giving Pain*

*Then The Song Was Ended, And I Realized Somehow*

*That Someway I Must Find You–And Say I Love You Now*

*That Always I Will Love You And Hold You In My Heart*

*Cause Sweetheart You're A Part Of Me, A Very Precious Part!*

*For Once, You Said–I Love You–I Love You Oh So Much*

*Those Words Reside, Within My Soul, My Very Life They Touch*

*I Think Of Them So Often, Hold Them Close When I Feel Blue*

*And Hope That You Remember, That I Once Spoke Them Too*

*That Somehow They Will Heal, The Anger And The Pain*

*And Once More We'll Be Together To Share Our Love Again*

*Share Each Precious Moment, Each Moment Yet To Live,*

*Receiving Love, And In Receiving, Lovingly To Give*

*Our Lives To One Another For Together We Belong*

*Together We Are Happy, Together We Are Strong*

*Together We Will Climb Mountains–We Could Not Climb Alone*

*And Share A Million Wondrous Dreams That We Alone Can Own*

*And If By Chance It Happens That They Don't All Come*
*True*
*We'll Dream Some More Each Moment*
*You're With Me–And I'm With You*
*Darling Listen To Me–I Love You Oh So Much*
*I Need You Back Within My Life*
*Your Love, Your Smile, Your Touch*

## USED TO BE

*I'm having trouble hanging on*
*Along with youth–The song is gone!*
*The Fairyland that used to be,*
*The dreamer child that once was me*
*Cursed by a witch forever more,*
*Banished to a barren shore,*
*Dressed in shrouds of endless pain*
*I cry–I thirst–then acid rain*
*Falls from up above*
*In agony my soul screams–Lord*
*Where is my land of Love?*
*Where gentle hands do reach out to help*
*Where sunshine fills the sky*
*Where once I dwelt in harmony*
*Until the rising tides*

*Of Hatred Born Of Passion*

*Deceitfulness from fear*

*Engulfed in while I slept*

*Then tides of bitter tears*

*Carried me so far away*

*To where there is no dawn of day*

*Far, from the place I once did dwell*

*To loneliness—a living hell*

*Where there's no you—and there's no me*

*And There's No Land—That Used To Be!*

*No rainbows arching cross the sky*

*No prisms shining bright,*

*No balloons—or wondrous stars*

*To brighten up the night*

*No music wafting softly*

*No dreams—no hope—no air*

*I kneel—submit—I cannot live*

*On black shores of despair!*

## VISIONS

*Visions That Haunt Me Thru The Night*

*Voices Crying Out Their Plight*

*And I! Tho I Care—What Can I Do?*

*Except Perhaps—To Pray For You!*

*But Then! Is There Anyone To Hear?*

*If So, Why Then, This Dreadful Fear?*

*This Helpless Feeling Deep Inside*

*That Makes Me Want To Run And Hide*

*But Where To Hide? Which Way To Go?*

*Confused! I Find–I Do Not Know!*

*For Tho I Sleep–The Dreams Go On*

*And In The Early Morning Dawn*

*The Dream They Call Reality*

*Takes His Daily Toll Of Me*

*So On And On Each Night And Day*

*Draining All My Life Away*

*And What Have I To Show?*

*What Does All This Furor Mean?*

*If Only I Could Know.*

## THE VISIT

*The Visit Was All Over*

*Nothing I Could Do Or Say*

*Would Stop The Hands Of Time*

*As The Minutes Ticked Away*

*One Last Embrace, A Rush Of Pain*

*Wondering When We'd Meet Again*

*I Watched You Go, Thru Tear Dimmed Eyes*

*And As Your Plane Began To Rise*

*My Soul Cried Out–Don't Go!*

*There's So Much More I Want To Say*

*Much More, I Need To Know!*

*And As I Watched, Until,*

*Your Plane Was Out Of Sight*

*I Thought, How Brief The Time,*

*In A Visit–As In Life*

*We Arrive! We Stay Awhile!*

*And Touch All Those We Know,*

*But Soon, The Visit's Over*

*And It's Time To Go.*

*But If We Love, And If We're Loved,*

*By Those We've Left Behind*

*Our Memories Will Ease The Pain*

*Until The Hands Of Time*

*Decree The Hour We Shall Meet*

*For Meet Again We Shall*

*The Bonds Of Love Can Conquer All,*

*The Very Gates Of Hell*

*Cannot Prevail Against It*

*If It Is Strong And True*

*So Tho You're Gone, We'll Meet Again*

*For God Knows, I Love You*

*And Tho Your Plane Has Disappeared*

*It Hasn't Really Gone*

*It's Just That I Can't See It*

*It Simply Has Gone On,*

*In Another Time Zone–To Another Place*

*Where Someone Waits To Meet You*

*Anxious To Embrace*

*All The Wondrous Things You Are*

*The Love You Have To Give,*

*The Purpose Of Your Visit*

*To Share The Life You Live*

*And If He's Wise He'll Understand*

*The Hands Of Time Move On*

*And Someday Just Like Me, He'll Find*

*The Time Has Gone*

*The Visit Will Be Over,*

*Nothing He Can Do Or Say*

*Will Change The Fact*

*The Time Has Come That You Must Go Away*

*But For A Time You'll Visit*

*And The Happiness You'll Share*

*Even When You're Gone,*

*Will Somehow Linger There,*

*Like The Memory Of Summer*

*And Of You–When You Were Here!*

Shirley Ann Wood

# WHAT ABOUT ME

*Some of what I am*

*Is part of what <u>you are</u>!*

*And I'll tell you how*

*Just how this came to be*

*First of all there's <u>who I am</u>*

*The way I <u>feel</u> and <u>think</u>*

*And then the way you touch and alter me!*

*Example*

*There's a day when I feel good*

*Everything is going as it should*

*Until we chance to meet*

*Accidentally - on the street*

*And you tell mw I'm not worthy!*

*If I <u>could,</u>*

*Just <u>change</u> a <u>little</u>.*

*You know! Here and there*

*Perhaps you'd find it*

*In your heart to care*

*<u>Perhaps</u> you'd love me then*

*In the meantime*

*You're a friend*

*So try a <u>little</u> harder, don't despair!*

*You smile and go your way*

*And I go mine*

*You feel so noble*

*True Friend, pure and fine!*

*Well friend, this heart is breaking*

*Deep inside*

*As I lift my chin and bite my lip*

*Trying hard to hide*

*The tears that well from deep inside of me!*

*If I am nothing in your eyes*

*What is there fore me?*

## WHAT GOOD

*What Good To See A Rose*

*A Rainbow Or A Stream*

*If There Is None To Share*

*The Beauty Or The Dream,*

*What Good To Believe, In Principles So True*

*To Live A Life Of Dedication*

*If It Begins And Ends With You*

*For Tho You May Believe*

*And Claim It For Your Own*

*You'll Walk The Path In Loneliness*

*Alone–So Much Alone*

*Knowing All The Loveliness That God Has Designed To
Give*

*Seeing With Your Heart And Soul*

*The Life That You Should Live*

*Of Trying As The Years Go By, To Impart All That You See*

*The Tender Things That Mean So Much To You*

*Should You Quit Or Go On Trying?*

*Brought To Your Knees You End Up Crying*

*Dear Lord God—I Wish I Knew What I Should Do*

*At This Point You Will Decide*

*And You'll Know Why Jesus Died*

*For All That He Believed In, Ceased To Be*

*Nothing On This Earth, Held Any Joy Or Worth*

*Except The Love He Had For You And Me*

*So He Drank The Bitter Cup, And Then He Offered Up*

*The Only Thing That He Had Left To Give*

*The Life That Was The Source*

*Of Belief—Of Love—The Force*

*That Should Be The Guiding Light To You And Me*

*And Tho The Light Is Bright—And Desperately I Call*

*I Hope—I Touch*

*But Thru My Fault—I Fall*

*Dear God—I Fall*

# WHAT I DIDN'T DO

*Dear Lord I ranted and raved, cried, whined*

*Pleaded and in general behaved*

*Like a spoiled bad tempered child*

*And I'm sorry – so sorry dear Lord!*

*I know and have known that you're just!*

*Yet I said that you cheated me*

*Denied and deceived me*

*And kicked up a terrible fuss*

*Now suddenly I've been able to see*

*I got everything I deserved*

*It was I cheated you by what I <u>didn't</u> do*


# WHEN

*I'll forget you when my heart no longer speaks your name*

*When Roses don't need sunshine*

*And Violets don't need rain*

*I'll forget you when this world*

*Has no more need of love*

*When the Sun and moon and Stars no longer shine above*

*Until then --*

*I'll just keep loving you*

*Tho it's all in vain*

*It seems my heart just can't let go-*

*Of the magic*

*That's your name!*

## WHERE BEAUTY LIVES

*True Beauty lives within the heart*

*Of one who loves you, see*

*I have beauty, strength and peace*

*Through your love for me*

*And so because of your great gift*

*I'll always be true*

*I return your gift of love–*

*Seven fold to you*

*Because you love me, I can give*

*Because you love me, I can live*

*As God would have me do*

*I can forsake all others–*

*Cleaving unto you*

*Together we're a power*

*Walking hand in hand*

*Love united–love with love–*

*We know and understand*

*The ones who seek, who are weak,*

*Who walk the path alone*

*They do not give, they cannot live*

With hearts as cold as stone–

For once–we were the very same

Knew the agony–the pain–

Of living without love

United, we personify

The power from above

That teaches us, not to betray

To deny, turn away–

From that which heaven gives

Our love for one another

In which all beauty lives

And so–because you love me

I give back my love to you

At least I would, if I just could

–Make what–I think–come true.

## WHERE DID I COME FROM

There are many answers to a question always asked

By each child "Where did I come from?" Then there is the
task

Of answering! Ah what to say? Confusion reigns supreme!

How to explain, get off the hook, yet somehow make it seem,

Acceptable?

First we hesitate–then try to look composed, wildly searching

*For the words–that heaven only knows*

*Might suffice, and then again, maybe they will not*

*To quell the curiosity of this tiny tot*

*Flower garden! Cabbage patch! I found you in a stream!*

*You were delivered by the stork, I got you from a dream,*

*I found you underneath a rock, an angel brought you here,*

*I got you with the groceries, while I was shopping dear,*

*Or being realistic, while quoting birth statistics*

*(So baby knows its not just you alone!)*

*There's the answer intellectual, that covers every sexual*

*Aspect of a birth that has been known!*

*The best answer that I've heard, was so many years ago*

*Spoken to a child in a voice so sweet and low,*

*As this mother cradled close her child then told the*

*story which beguiled and brought forth a dimpled smile*

*As she said–of course I'll tell you–For it was a long, long*

*while*

*Before our prayers were answered and you came to be*

*Until that day there was no you–just your Dad and me*

*But we knew someday you'd come for Honey don't you*

*know*

*I loved your Daddy very much and your Daddy loved me, so*

*Since we were here because of love, I knew that God would*

*see*

*That because of His great love, You'd simply have to be*

*For that is where we came from, the power known as love,*

*And, in the beginning–our great God up above*

*Arranged things with that thought in mind, and to this very day*

*Babies are made from Moms and Dads with God to help along the way.*

*I'll tell you more when you are older–but Daddies plant a seed*

*In Mommies who carry a tiny egg that very greatly need*

*To blend together with the seed so a baby then can start*

*To grow within her tummy (right next to Mommy's heart)*

*And after months of waiting the baby then is born*

*The doctor helps it to arrive–then wraps it up real warm*

*And everyone is so excited, for it's a magic time*

*I know that I was happy, that you were Dad's and Mine*

*For you were oh so special–and as I held you dear,*

*My heart was full of Thanks for Love, the reason you are here.*

## WHERE DID SHIRLEY GO

*Dear God I Am Concerned–So Really Need To Know*

*What's Happened To The One "I Am" And Where Did Shirley Go?*

*For You Created Me "To Be!" Within Your Plan–Your Time*

*Unique–As Are, All Others–In Your Holy Mind!*

*Yet From Time To Time We Leave You–Take Form On Planet*
*Earth*

*Eternal Souls In Mortal Bodies, Struggling From Birth*

*To Survive–To Understand–Where We Fit Within Your Plan,*

*Resisting Those Who Mold Us, To Their Ways, Their Will*

*Yet In Spite Of All Our Efforts–Being Molded Still!*

*Why All Of This? What Does It Mean?*

*Why Bother Then To Hope–To Dream?*

*If We Cannot Fulfill Any–But Another's Dream*

*Broken By Their Will!*

*Because Their Will Is Stronger*

*By Force It Often Overrides*

*"Love" Your First Commandment*

*As It Mocks, Rejects, Divides*

*This "Weakness" We Who Love Call Strength*

*Yet Is This Really So? If It Is, What Of My Efforts*

*And Where Did Shirley Go!*

## WHERE YELLOW ROSES GROW

*There is a world somewhere–I know!*

*My world–Where Yellow Roses Grow*

*Where people laugh, but never cry,*

*Where rainbows arch across the sky!*

*This wondrous world, I've never seen*

*Except sometimes–when ere I dream,*

*Is like a wish–or Fantasy*

*A world that very few can see*

*And yet--It seems so real to me!*

*There are crystal waterfalls,*

*And Love Is Ruler Over All,*

*Each day is filled with promise*

*Then when the day is stilled,*

*Each night becomes enchantment,*

*All promises fulfilled!*

*There are no demons living there,*

*No pain, no death, no deep despair,*

*No deceit, nor hopeless sighs,*

*For Hatred, lust, and pointless lies*

*That grow in hearts unseen*

*Have no place–within my world*

*This world–called "Just a Dream"*

*They think I can reach–Too high–"I know!"*

*But someday soon–I'll leave–and go*

*To where my Yellow Roses grow*

*To where my heart has ever been*

*Since the moment of my birth,*

*And kept my soul from finding–A home*

*On Planet Earth!*

*Soft dreams shall enfold me,*

*Then give me leave to go,*

*Back to my world—from whence I came*

*Where Yellow Roses Grow!*

## WHY

*I wish I knew Why*

*My highs are so high*

*My lows are so low*

*Why I am I!*

*I've tried <u>so</u> hard to be*

*Anybody but me*

*To alter the path*

*They call destiny*

*I've <u>used</u> every trick in the book*

*Known to man*

*But try as I will or hard as I can*

*I cannot escape the one that I am*

*I wanted so much for the one I call me*

*Whatever was great I wanted to be*

*Understanding and loyal, brilliant and true*

*Compassionate, loving, with great humor too*

*The best there can be in body and mind*

*Representing the virtues of God in mankind*

*But it seems at my best*

*I am nothing at all*

*Bone weary I'll climb – only to fall*

*Betrayed, I find, in turn I betray*

*Unloved, I get even by walking away*

*Angry and brooding, head yet unbowed*

*Another day looming, apart from the crowd*

*I survey all the years that have passed quickly by*

*And somewhere inside me*

*A child starts to cry*

*The cry is so tiny, frightened, alone*

*Innocence pulled from its truth and its home*

*Taken from where it was once*

*Pure and free*

*Caged deep inside what I've*

*Come to be*

*I listen a moment*

*To what used to be me!*

*I reach deep inside to quell the small cry*

*And as I reach down I notice the sky*

*Has darkened, nighttime is here*

*And I and the child huddle close*

*In our fear*

*Together we sense our lifetime is done*

We'll never more feel the warmth of the sun

I ask her forgiveness that she could not be

She was <u>just</u> not enough to satisfy me

But she was so strong, so sweet and so wise

So blessed, so loved, in God's holy eyes

I knew in my heart I must keep her with me

A prisoner inside so the world could not see

The beauty, the love, she could share

She could be

If it were not for the pride and desire of me

Forgive me – my Father for what I have done

Turning my back on your truth and your Son (Sun)

My lifetime is ending

I've wasted it all

And now as eternity's starting to fall

I know that the child I kept deep inside

The one I denied, that I tried to hide

Held all of the keys to what <u>I</u> should have been

Why did I search outward

Instead of within

Now that it's too late

I look in and I see

All that I was – that you meant me to be

It's right that I perish but let the child live

*Out of darkness I lift her and to you I now give*

*The small lovely part of this person called me*

*Take her home, make her strong*

*And then set her free*

*To become all the things*

*That you meant her to be!*


## WITHOUT LOVE

*If there's no sun the world is cold and bare and bleak and dark*

*If there's no love such bleakness settles deep within the heart*

*Still the human spirit struggles in this unnatural state*

*Even " knowing " – without love, already it's too late–*

*It drives the coldness and frantically persists*

*Seeking worth of any kind – a glance – a touch – a kiss*


## WOMAN OF THE EARTH

*I am a woman of the earth, who's tasted life and death and birth*

*Why does my spirit yearn?*

*What makes me long? What makes me search? A simple woman of the earth*

*Why does my spirit burn?*

To know such things, that on this earth, <u>may</u> not be revealed

Power lost in ages past, <u>Secrets</u> now concealed–

Why am I so restless? Why do I hunger as I eat?

What makes me stand – the conqueror! – Even in defeat?

What makes me care? – Or not at all?

A paradox – so small – yet tall! –Is there a secret key?

That will unlock the vault of time and solve this mystery?

How come I to this body? That dwells on planet Earth!

Exiled from my source of joy. The mighty universe!

From whence it seems – I traveled – so very long ago

To this world, wherein I dwell! Yet – I do not know!

There is little in this place – less! – within the human race

That appeals to me! I loath the ties, deceit and lies–

The dreadful cruelty – that far surpasses and outweighs

The little good I've seen, and makes the words

Of God above – some distant crazy dream!

So it has been – since time began – so it will ever be!

Until – our Lord returns to earth – to set his people free!

Only then – will Spirits rest – cease their endless thirsting quest–

For Eden! Source of man! To <u>be</u> once more – what once

We were, when the world began!

To feel once more the blessing – to shed this ugly curse,

That makes me wish I'd not been born – A woman of the earth

# WOOD 'N DOLL

*There once was a girl who was made of wood*

*Like a slender willow tree*

*She bowed to the storms and bent to the breeze*

*And longed all her life to be free*

*She wanted to wander the face of the earth*

*To discover her failings, her talent, her worth*

*But her branches gave shelter to the lost and forlorn*

*And her roots from the earth just couldn't be torn*

*So she grew ever taller, the one way to go*

*Reaching towards heaven, Its secrets to know*

*Then came the woodsman with axe sharp and keen*

*He cut thru her heart and ended that dream*

*Thrown in the river, tumbled and tossed*

*She was like driftwood, useless and lost*

*Then she was lifted and transformed by man*

*A new shape was formed, a new life began*

*A puppet, performing for one and all*

*The manipulated, heartbroken*

*Wood 'n Doll*

# WORDS

*The magic carpet–that transports the mind*

*To Elysian shores of joy–WHEN–The words are kind*

Ah! But when they are unkind–like a distant tolling bell,

They sadden, heart and soul and mind

As they sound their final knoll,

Words, The Power–yours the choice

Which to discard–which to voice.

As you speak–"So it shall be" to another's mind

"You"–Create the memory–loving, or, unkind

"With Words!"


# YESTERDAY

Yesterday and Yesterday and Yesterday and Yesterday

I heard you say, and <u>you</u> say, and <u>you</u> say, and <u>you</u> say

Thank you – you have eased my mind

Helped me so – your words are kind

Your manner soothing, voice so calm

Feel better now – I can go on

And you went on. Where did you go?

When <u>I</u> cried out – I need you so!

Not repayment, just a need.

That you will hear, that you will heed,

The cry that comes from deep inside

Where all my terrors live

The secret place where people hide

When others can – or will not give

*Just a word, just a moment*

*In the span of time*

*It takes so <u>little</u> Caring to ease a troubled mind,*

*Can you not see that those who Love you*

*Make easier your way?*

*They will not fail, or ever doubt you*

*What' ere you do or say?*

*But they are human just like you,*

*And have their tribulation too!*

*When They reach out. What will you say*

*Will you remember Yesterday*

*Yesterday – Yesterday*

*Yesterday*

## YOU

*I knew you once–when you were young,*

*Compassionate and true*

*Filled with Life, filled with Love,*

*Daring to be you*

*In spite of all–your laughter rang*

*Strong–your will–"To Be"*

*Enfolding all, with your great Love*

*You touched the soul of me*

*I longed to have you by my side,*

*To share your deep desires,*

*But–not to be–this heartfelt dream*

*For suddenly the fire*

*That once was you, began to die*

*Then slowly ceased to be!*

*There was none, to mourn the loss*

*Unless you counted me!*

*It seems they never noticed*

*The fading of your light*

*But perhaps it was because,*

*They dwelt within the night!*

*They taught you all the things they knew,*

*Killing all that once was you!*

*Now you are old–the years have gone,*

*But deep within my heart, the song*

*Of Love–That Used To Be*

*Brings back the Vision of the World,*

*That you once offered me!*

*Then the tears I've shed so long*

*For dreams long held, and years long gone*

*Bed in what used to be,*

*And I return with aching heart*

*To now! Reality!*

*A place without you–all alone*

*No dreams–no love–just me!*

# YOU!

*The other day you spoke to me*

*Of all the things you'd like to be*

*Well all these things are what I see*

*When I look at you!*

*All the wondrous deeds you spoke of*

*These are what you do!*

*So still your fears that passing years*

*Will somehow conquer you*

*Thru God – thru love*

*Thru faith and works*

*You've made some dreams come true*

*And there are more – a treasure store*

*Of wonders yet to be*

*You have only to believe*

*In their reality!*

*For you are special – gifted*

*Gentle, kind and good!*

*So all your world is forming now*

*Exactly as it should!*

*And all the good things that you do*

*Shall in turn come back to you*

*This is a certainty!*

*For in your heart no malice lives*

*No greed – no jealousy*

*To those you touch*

*You give so much*

*It's very plain to see*

*That you are all*

*And more – much more*

*Than all you'd like to be!*

## YOU WILL NEVER KNOW

*You will never know my love–just what you mean to me*

*For barriers of time my love, dictate this cannot be!*

*If I could–love–you must know–I would change*

*The status quo!*

*I would change with my own will*

*The portent we call time*

*Speed up your years–delay my own*

*So then you could be mine*

*Then I would do for you my love–what you have done for me*

*But alas I cannot change what is, and what will be*

*But there is on thing I can do! With deep regard and love for*

*you*

*And that is–walk away! Tho I would–if*

*I just could, embrace your love–and stay!*

*For you are all a man could be–A person set apart*

*A man of pure nobility–sweet–gentle–loving heart!*